Managing Company Growth

Managing Company Growth

Coopers & Lybrand Deloitte

Butterworths
London, Dublin, Edinburgh
1990

United Kingdom	Butterworth & Co (Publishers) Ltd, 88 Kingsway, LONDON WC2B 6AB and 4 Hill Street, EDINBURGH EH2 3JZ
Australia	Butterworths Pty Ltd, SYDNEY, MELBOURNE, BRISBANE, ADELAIDE, PERTH, CANBERRA and HOBART
Canada	Butterworths Canada Ltd, TORONTO and VANCOUVER
Ireland	Butterworth (Ireland) Ltd, DUBLIN
Malaysia	Malayan Law Journal Sdn Bhd, KUALA LUMPUR
New Zealand	Butterworths of New Zealand Ltd, WELLINGTON and AUCKLAND
Puerto Rico	Equity de Puerto Rico, Inc, HATO REY
Singapore	Malayan Law Journal Pte Ltd, SINGAPORE
USA	Butterworth Legal Publishers, AUSTIN, Texas; BOSTON, Massachusetts; CLEARWATER, Florida (D & S Publishers); ORFORD, New Hampshire (Equity Publishing); ST PAUL, Minnesota; and SEATTLE, Washington

A CIP Catalogue record for this book is available from the British Library.

ISBN 0 406 67821 9

Printed and bound in Great Britain by Mackays of Chatham PLC, Kent

Preface

This book has been written to address a need that we at Coopers & Lybrand Deloitte have perceived in advising growing businesses for many years.

Managers of growing businesses and their advisors require a working knowledge of a number of disciplines including strategic planning, information systems, finance, tax, marketing, operations and personnel management. It is clear that the talents demanded of managers and their advisors cover a broad range of skills. This book aims to provide them with an introduction to each of these skill requirements so that development of the company can continue and also to provide a guide through the changes which will inevitably accompany growth.

As a first step in the development of their business, entrepreneurs need to formulate a strategy for growth which should be documented in a business plan. In addition, they should establish management information systems to monitor progress and thereby impose control over operations. These disciplines are also necessary if managers are to exploit fully the available internal sources of funds and, if appropriate, attract a potential outside provider of finance to support the business. The first two chapters of this book provide a framework for the development of a corporate plan and management information systems; while Chapter 3 gives guidance on working capital management and appropriate external sources of finance to suit the needs of the growing business.

Chapter 4 reviews the taxation considerations of importance to the growing company, its shareholders and employees and provides tax planning points for companies seeking to expand through corporate acquisitions.

Chapter 5 explains the role of marketing in sustaining competitive advantage and focuses on the implications of growth for marketing action and strategy. The marketing function must involve the whole company in examining and understanding what the customer requires. This point is developed in the following chapter on 'operations', which embraces the establishment of customer needs and the effective management of customer service, suppliers and quality. Companies that address these issues successfully gain a major advantage in attracting and retaining the best employees, since care for the customer is complementary to care for the employee. Moreover, the effective management of personnel is fundamental to the continued success of the business. Human resource issues are considered in Chapter 7, with particular emphasis on recruitment, remuneration and retention.

The need to involve employees in planning is highlighted in the final chapter, 'Building on Growth', where corporate acquisitions are discussed. The advantages of corporate acquisitions to enhance growth are acknowledged by most entrepreneurs. Not all, however, develop an acquisition strategy to ensure that this path is followed in a co-ordinated and considered fashion. This chapter provides a useful guide to the development of an acquisitions strategy and to the considerations necessary when valuing a target company.

For the corporate manager who wants his business to thrive, this book is an invaluable source of guidance for corporate planning, problem solving, and decision making.

Richard P Murphy
Coopers & Lybrand Deloitte

The Authors

This book has been written by partners and professional staff of Coopers & Lybrand Deloitte, all of whom are experienced in working with and advising growing companies and entrepreneurial management teams.

The contributors, who were drawn from the Business Services, Taxation and Management Consultancy practices of Coopers & Lybrand Deloitte, were:

Alistair J B Rose
Wilson W Jennings
Frank W Milton
David W Cartwright
Phil Collinge
Kevin J Forsyth

In addition, the following Coopers & Lybrand Deloitte professionals provided invaluable advice and assistance: Richard Murphy, Chris Maw, Duncan Ralph, Bill Rayment, Stephen Bailey, Peter Hill, Caroline Spicer and Ron Nattrass.

The authors wish to thank Financial Services Management Development Limited (FSMD) and, in particular, Robert Rosenfeld and Kevin Jagiello for their co-operation in providing material used in Chapter 1.

Contents

Introduction

There are many cautionary tales of apparently successful companies and entrepreneurs that were, in the final analysis, unable to cope with the demands of company growth. Failure may have been due to one or more of a multitude of potential pitfalls including, a lack of strategy, under-capitalisation, inflexibility, poor recruitment and so on. Expansion is often the most difficult and dangerous step the smaller business will take and as a result successful management of this phase is often the most important in a company's development.

Growth is a generic term used by many companies to define their corporate objective. This will usually encompass a number of goals such as increased market share, rising profitability, enhanced earnings per share, higher dividends and many others. In this book we seek to discuss and develop the broad concepts and management disciplines that must be considered by the growing business if such targets are to be successfully achieved.

The type of organisation intended to benefit from the concepts discussed is one that has successfully mastered the first phase of growth from its inception and is now seeking to develop the second phase. This may involve, for example, the launch of new products, entry into new markets, both domestic and overseas, or enhancement of production and distribution resources.

Not only must the entrepreneur understand the additional demands arising if growth is to be successfully achieved and consolidated upon, but also he must anticipate the changes which growth will bring, and take action to prepare the company for expansion in good time. It is obvious that if an organisation is to be managed successfully then, for example, suitable management information systems are required. Such systems cannot be created overnight and require planning and implementation over a period so that they actually assist the growth process. Recognition of the need to implement systems and disciplines such as these is frequently made at too late a stage in the growth process.

The traditional entrepreneur will have a background in sales or marketing or occasionally production. He has the know-how for the production process or the techniques to sell his product or services. He is unlikely, however, to be experienced in financial and administrative matters. Moreover, it would be unrealistic to expect this one individual to have all the necessary financial, legal, accounting and administrative skills that are required to manage a successful business operation.

A company's ability to grow in volume terms may, ironically, result in the entrepreneur being confronted by too much success, too quickly; for example, sales growth achieved without a corresponding increase in profitability and/or cash flow due to variable pricing, increased overheads or excessive stockholding. Administrative and financial controls are required if profits and growth are to be maximised. Whilst one would not expect the entrepreneur necessarily to become an expert in finance or administrative matters, he should at least develop a working knowledge of these areas. This book should alert the entrepreneur to those wider issues which are fundamental to the continued success of the business.

Having said that the entrepreneur should develop a working knowledge of a number of broad concepts discussed in this book; so is the case for the advisor to the growing company. Accountants and other advisors, such as bankers and lawyers, who work with the entrepreneur must recognise that it is impossible to serve the growing business without an understanding of the aspirations of the owner-manager. Having obtained this knowledge, and established a close professional relationship, the advisor is well placed to ensure that the entrepreneur avoids the potential pitfalls awaiting the unwary. Accordingly, the concepts and disciplines detailed in this book are also those that should be understood and developed by the growing company's professional advisor. The advisor has an important role in assisting the entrepreneur in planning and implementing the early stages of growth. Ultimately, the successful growing company should be in a position to develop systems and strategies through its own internal resources, however until then, the advisor has a key role in anticipating the disciplines and resources required if the successful first phase of growth is to be consolidated and developed further.

One of the key elements emphasised throughout the book is the need to plan; and in particular, long-term profitability is impossible without adequate financial planning. The typical emerging business will be thinly capitalised and highly geared which, combined with limited personnel and managerial resources, results in difficulties in continuing the current scale of operations, let alone undertaking growth.

The problems faced by the growing company may be compounded by economic factors such as interest rate changes and exchange rate movements. For the entrepreneur to survive under these conditions then growth must be planned and co-ordinated in a disciplined manner. Frequently we see business failures arise through inadequate financial management.

The foundation of financial management is information. Comprehensive information is the basis upon which day-to-day operations are controlled but it is also the platform for the business planning process. The business strategy and financial plans should give direction to corporate decision making. We frequently encounter companies that allocate considerable resources to the compilation of a business plan only to discard it for the purposes of day-to-day decision making. It is important for the entrepreneur to use his plan as a guide for measuring ongoing operations and, in particular, to monitor variations from planned objectives. In this way companies will be in a position to take remedial action to accomplish their profit objectives. As the business grows, so the entrepreneur should be concerned only with variations to the strategy and plan, as he cannot expect to cover all aspects of the company as it expands.

There are entrepreneurs who have successfully built their business to significant volumes without instituting the financial controls and other management procedures necessary to achieve their final objectives.

However, at some stage they have discovered that growth without planning and financial control can lead to disaster.

The topics discussed in the book are generally applicable to manufacturing or service industries. However, to avoid continual repetition of the phrase 'product or service' all references are to 'product'. It should be readily apparent when a particular point applies only to a product as opposed to a service.

This book is correct to the best of our knowledge and belief at the time of going to press. Its application to particular situations will depend on the circumstances involved. It is recommended that specific advice is sought before any action is taken.

CHAPTER 1

Corporate Planning

Introduction

One of the key functions of corporate planning is to ensure that the policies of a company are co-ordinated and focused toward a single set of objectives. This may only be achieved, however, if a *corporate strategy* is explicitly developed through a formalised planning process, otherwise the company risks facing a loss of direction as managers follow their own individual goals.

Corporate strategy is concerned with the means by which resources will be allocated to achieve competitive advantage so as to generate increasing financial returns. Strategy can be defined as the integrated process of management which combines the objectives or goals of the business with its plans and tactics; it therefore provides the link between the ends and the means of achieving those ends. In short, strategy assists the company in competing successfully.

Strategy is about effectiveness—deciding the right things to do—rather than about efficiency—deciding how to do things correctly. The latter is the concern of operational planning. Developing a strategy requires determining the overall purpose of a business; where it wants to be in five, ten or more years time and how it intends to get there. Strategy is concerned with certain central questions:

- what activities should form the business' operations?
- what in market and competitive terms should be the objectives?
- how should the business be organised to:
  —concentrate resources on the determinants of competitive advantage?
  —create an environment oriented to achievement?

Strategy is more concerned with direction and thrust than with precision.

In addition, the notion of strategy exists at two levels—for the business as a whole, and for the individual functions or operations within the business. The former is often called corporate, business or competitive strategy, while the latter is referred to as marketing strategy, manufacturing strategy etc. This chapter is primarily concerned with business strategy; other chapters deal with specific operational areas.

The link between the two levels can be elegantly illustrated by the 'wheel of strategy', developed in the 1970s by Andrews, Christensen and others in the Policy Group of the Harvard Business School.

In Fig 1.1 opposite, the business strategy (the ends and the means) forms the hub and the operational activities of the company the spokes. The

Fig 1.1: The Wheel of Strategy

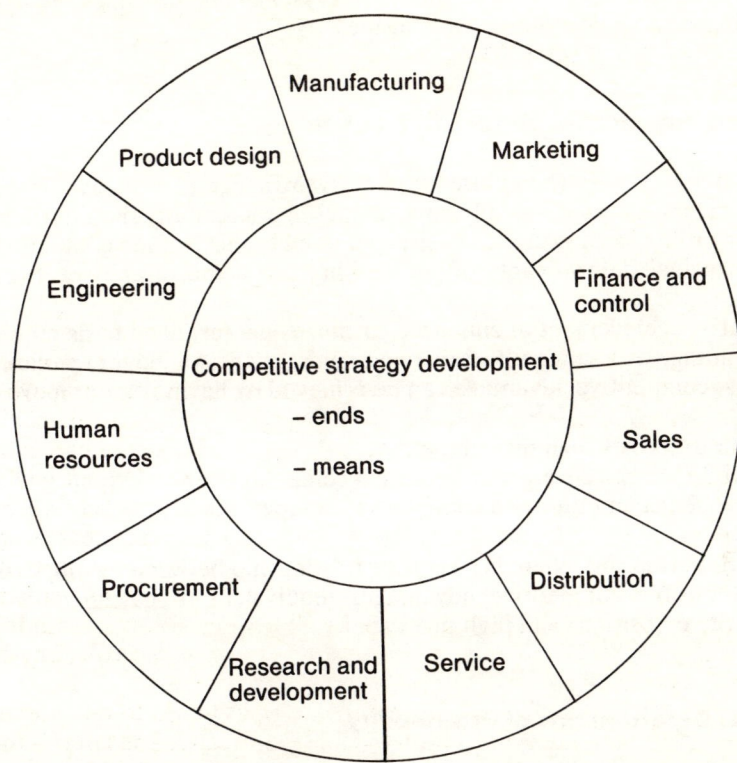

spokes radiate from the hub, and take their place in relation to each other since they are fixed to the hub. Without the hub, the wheel would collapse. Equally, the wheel would collapse if a spoke was weak or missing. This seeks to illustrate that successful businesses establish a strategy and then ensure that the operational activities carried out are consistent with that strategy and with each other, and also, that the business as a whole is only as strong as its weakest operational link.

A final point is that strategy is often, particularly in smaller businesses, not instantly visible. Rather than being embodied in a 'Strategic Plan', strategy may only be discernible as a pattern arising from a stream of decisions. It is therefore more likely to take an evolutionary path, rather than a revolutionary one. It does not matter, necessarily, if the strategy is not documented, although there are sound reasons for doing so in most businesses (discussed later). What is important, however, is that if there is no strategy, there will be no pattern to the decision making process. The reasons for having a strategy, however informal, ought to be clear to all businessmen operating in a competitive environment which is subject to an increasing degree of change.

The purpose of this chapter is to establish a means for developing a strategy to manage and enhance growth built upon an analysis of industry and competition. The chapter will introduce some of the key concepts used in strategic analysis by companies and provides a set of tools and perspectives to highlight key areas in the evaluation of business development opportunities. The final part of the chapter gives guidance on the documentation of corporate strategy within a business plan and discusses the issues affecting strategy for the growing business.

The importance of competitive advantage

As the definition of strategy already put forward suggests, strategy forms the basis of competing successfully, and competing successfully should result in greater profits, on a sustained basis, compared to those of the competition. The principal determinants of profitability are demonstrated by Fig 1.2 below.

Clearly, achievement of enhanced earnings on a sustained basis requires an advantage over competitors on one or more of the component variables.

Thus, competitive advantage can be achieved by having one or more of:

- lower unit costs than the competition
- an ability to realise higher prices than competitors
- enhanced asset utilisation compared to competitors.

Stemming from this, there is a positive relationship between having strong and defensible competitive advantages (equivalent to having a strong competitive position) and high profitability.

Fig 1.2: Determinants of Profitability

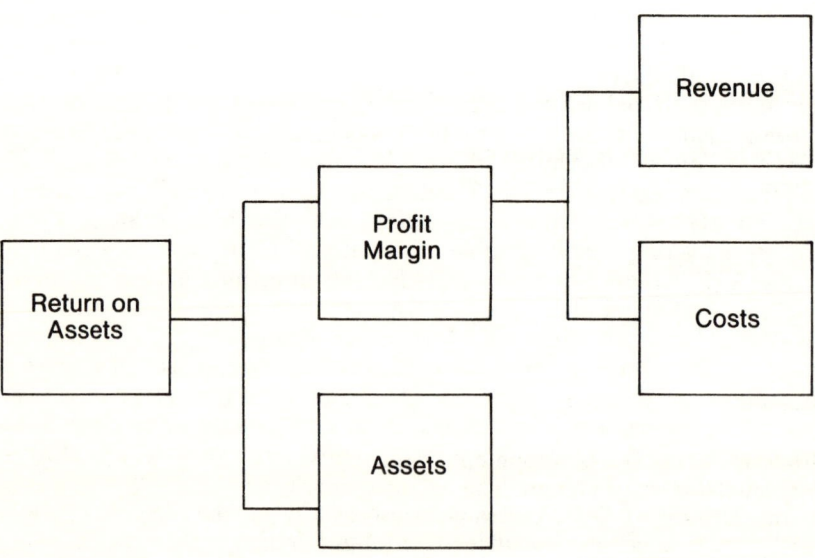

Achievement of competitive advantage

The key to strategy appears to be simple; gaining sustainable economic advantage over one's competitors. In practice, of course, it is not so simple or everyone would achieve it. The basis for 'defensible advantage' is specific to each area of business and requires careful competitive and industry analysis to identify a company's strengths, weaknesses, opportunities and threats. For example:

- in mining (where there is little opportunity to impact on price realisation because of the free market) relative cost position, as determined by location, scale and quality, becomes the key determinant of final profitability
- in businesses where economies of scale are significant, eg the volume car industry, the relative cost position is also crucial
- in retailing, relative cost (eg from location or purchasing) can be the determining factor, or alternatively asset utilisation (sales/sq ft, debtors, creditors and inventory management) may be the key variable.

In many industries and markets, the differing requirements of distinct and homogeneous customer groups provide opportunities for success through the process of market segmentation. Competitors may focus on the needs of specific segments and attempt to satisfy these, ie provide them with 'value', as opposed to the 'generalists' who supply the whole market. In this way competitors may achieve higher prices without necessarily incurring higher costs. A weak generalist competitor can attempt to achieve an advantage by segmenting the market to gain a stronger position in a new segment.

A first requirement, therefore, for developing a strategy has to be a detailed understanding of how competitive advantage can be built and sustained in the market. This requires analysis of the market characteristics, of competitive behaviour and economics, and of market segmentation.

Analysis of industry and competition

Several tools and perspectives have been developed to provide a framework for the analysis of any industry or market sector; these include:

1. the environments matrix
2. the product portfolio matrix
3. the market life cycle chart
4. Porter's model of competitive analysis.

The environments matrix

The first step in the development of a competitive strategy is relating the company to its environment. The environments matrix (see Fig 1.3 on page 8) categorises the market environment into four basic types on two criteria:

1. potential sources of competitive approach to the market—few or many
2. size of advantage that can be attained vis-a-vis the competition—large or small.

Fig 1.3: The Environments Matrix

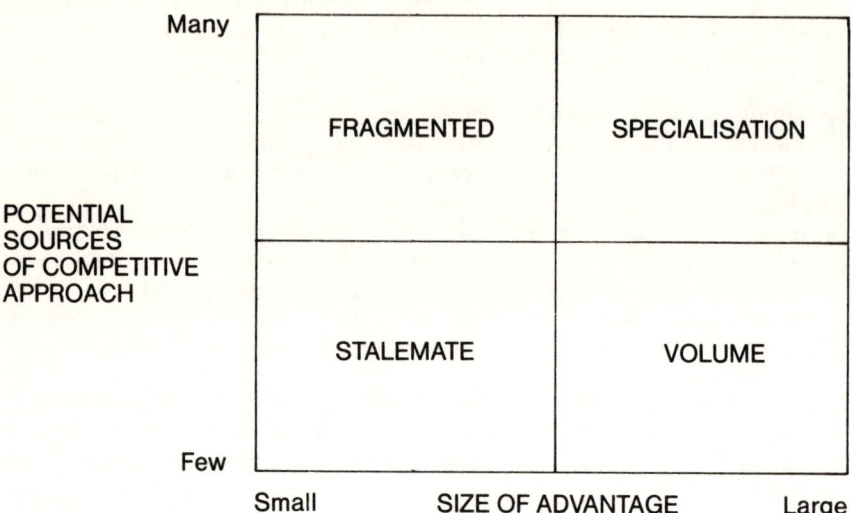

Characteristics of each market type and the key factors for success are:

Fragmented   In this market there are a wide variety of competitors and products on offer. The businesses are usually labour intensive and product development is through incremental innovation. In addition, there will be low entry costs, small investment requirements and the companies will be working capital driven.

Typical participants in this market are cottage industries or local services such as corner shops, restaurants, garages. Private sector construction may also be classified under this heading.

The key strategies for success in this market are based on a responsive and opportunistic approach demanding fast, fluid, flexible and short-term tactics. Reactive and adaptive to market needs, the business must achieve high utilisation rates from its employees. Management systems are normally decentralised.

Specialisation   This is a small, well-defined market with few competitors. The business is driven by an emphasis on quality and the need to offer good value. Typically, expenditure on personnel (wages, training etc) will be high.

Participants in this market will include niche retailers, suppliers of designer goods, training and consultancy companies and high class hotels.

In order to succeed in this environment the business must adopt a strategy which provides management with the best understanding of their customer needs. Since quality is crucial the company should strive to be 'better than the best' through, for example, continual R & D expenditure. Human resource issues are critical if the skill base is to be protected. Control will best be achieved through an integrated cell structure.

Stalemate   This is a large, basic or mature market often dealing in commodity products. There is usually no dominant company, and all participants are established businesses. A large investment in resources is required and entry costs are high. Pricing and profitability are determined by the state of the economy generally. There are no further economies of scale available.

Participants in this sector include the oil industry and retail banking.

The key factors for success, which should thus determine strategy, are high asset productivity linked to competitive price 'understandings' to protect the present position of the business. Control is best effected over tight short spans.

Volume   This is a mass market of standardised product with few dominant competitors and operating with streamlined and large distribution channels. There are high marketing costs with diminishing returns but large economies of scale and with opportunities for shared costs across product ranges.

Typical volume industries include motor cars, mainframe computers, photocopiers, petfood and tobacco industries.

The corporate strategy in a volume market should aim for market dominance with a high commitment to expenditure on resources. Profitability horizons will be long term. Access to distribution channels is fundamental and key decisions are taken centrally.

It is clear from the above analysis that the strategies for success differ between market place environments. Moreover, the potential profits are also different. Volume and specialisation markets will generate large profits and high margins respectively; while fragmented and stalemate markets yield only small profits and low margins in the long run.

In formulating a strategy for growth, management will typically consider four possibilities:

1. increased market penetration
2. further product development
3. market development
4. diversification.

Whichever of these routes is chosen, it is essential to be clear about the nature of the environment in which the company will be operating so that the most appropriate strategy is selected. Clearly, for market penetration and product development, existing strategies may suffice; whereas market development and diversification may involve a movement on the environments matrix and so new strategies may be required.

WIDER ENVIRONMENTAL ISSUES

In addition to the market environment, as discussed above, there are other, wider environmental issues which ought to be addressed in the formulation of corporate strategy. These are summarised in Fig 1.4 (page 10).

Fig 1.4: Potentially Significant Environmental Variables

Economic Conditions	Demographic Trends	Technological Changes	Social-Cultural Factors	Political-Legal Factors
GNP trends	Growth rate of population	Government spending on R & D	Lifestyle changes	Environment protection laws
Interest rates	Age distribution	Industry spending on R & D	Career expectations	Changes to tax laws
Money supply	Regional shifts of population	Focus of technological efforts	Consumer activism	Special incentives
Inflation rates	Life expectancies	Patent protection	Ecological considerations	Foreign trade regulations
Unemployment levels	Birth rates			
Wage/price controls				
Exchange rates				
Energy availability				

A detailed analysis of these issues is beyond the scope of this book. Suffice to say that there are three key issues which will need to be addressed in the formulation of the corporate strategy:

1. is the current strategy of the business consistent with the external environment?
2. what new opportunities and threats will arise as a result of changes in the external environment?
3. what action is required to protect/enhance the company's position?

In short, management must take into account wider environmental considerations and anticipate, within their strategy, the impact of future environmental considerations upon demand and the cost of supply.

The product portfolio matrix (PPM)

The PPM is built upon the theory that a large market share will produce greater levels of profit than a small share of the market. Underlying this is the assumption that management is able to break down the company into its constituent parts so as to assess the competitive position in each sector in which the company operates. Each part (product) is assessed on two criteria (see Fig 1.5 below):

1. growth rate
2. market share.

Fig 1.5: The Product Portfolio Matrix (Boston Consulting Group)

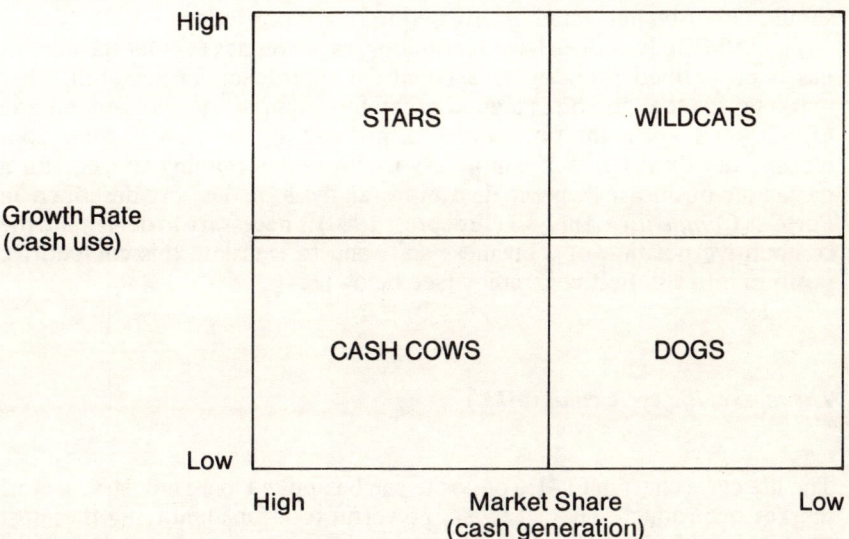

'Stars'—operate in high growth sectors with large market share.
'Dogs'—have small market share in low growth sectors.
'Cash Cows'—have large market share in low growth businesses. Cash Cows provide the stable earnings base which supports the firm.
'Wildcats'—this category consists of products with a low share of a high growth business.

Wildcat products have the best opportunity of becoming the Stars of the future, however they require large injections of cash to finance the research, development and marketing expenditure required to increase their market share.

Stars generate cash, although this is required to service the growth in the market that is experienced in this sector; consequently, although highly profitable, Stars generate modest cash flows.

Cash Cows operate in mature markets where there is low growth. They may have been yesterday's Stars and provide the stable earnings base which supports the company. The large positive cash flows generated by Cash Cows may be used to fund the Wildcat products so that they may become Stars.

Once growth reduces in the sector in which a Star operates, the Star becomes a Cash Cow which can then be used to finance new Wildcat products, and so the cycle continues.

The location of a business' products on the portfolio matrix is indicative of the current health of a portfolio. The ideal portfolio would consist of a mix of Stars and Cash Cows.

The decision about which Wildcats to invest in to build into Stars becomes a key strategic one. Wildcats which are not chosen for investment should be 'harvested' (managed to generate cash) until they become Dogs. Dogs should either be harvested or divested from the portfolio.

The PPM analysis does have limitations, as it assumes (a) that the market has been defined properly to account for interdependencies with other markets, (b) that growth is a good proxy for required cash investment and (c) market share is the final source of profitability. In view of these conditions, the PPM by itself is not very useful in determining strategy for a particular business. A great deal more analysis of the sort described in Porter's *Competitive Analysis* (Freepress 1980) is necessary to determine the competitive position of a business unit, and to translate this competitive position into a definitive strategy (see below).

The market life cycle chart (MLC)

The life cycle chart in Fig 1.6 opposite can be applied to an industry, sector, market or product. The MLC is a powerful tool for identifying the most appropriate strategies for the business. As the business advances through its life cycle, the nature of competition will change. Once the current position of the business has been plotted on the chart it is possible to adopt focused strategies so that opportunities are exploited and threats mitigated.

Fig 1.6: The Market Life Cycle Chart
(see M E Porter, Competitive Strategy, 1980, Freepress)

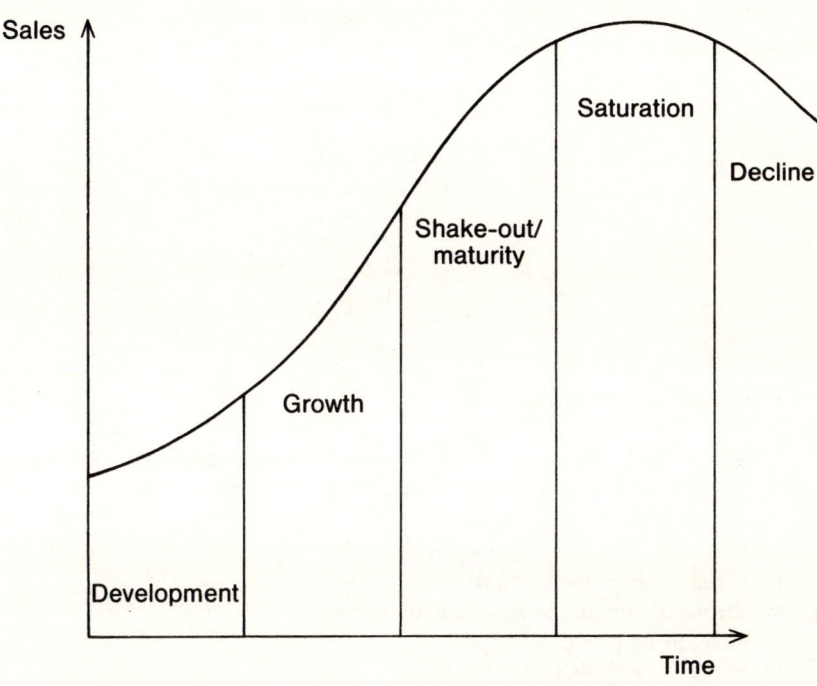

KEY STRATEGIES FOR DIFFERENT STAGES OF THE LIFE CYCLE

Life cycle stage	*Appropriate strategies*
1. Development	1. the functional emphasis will be on research and development
	2. strategy should be geared towards education of customers and encouragement of product utilisation
	3. product quality should be maintained by the rapid correction of any defects.
2. Growth	1. emphasis on brand management skills
	2. development of distribution systems
	3. build-up of productive capacity
	4. generation of cash, fund raising and investment in resources.
3. Shake-out	1. development of dealer relationships
	2. development of customer loyalty and perceptions.

4. Maturity
    1. enhancement of brand name
    2. improved communication and promotion
    3. improved distribution
    4. improved product
    5. exploit cost advantages.

5. Saturation
    1. manage to generate cash (harvest)
    2. minimisation of costs
    3. sale of redundant assets.

6. Decline
    1. control costs
    2. employ exit strategies
        (a) alternative use/sale of production facilities
        (b) sale of business as a 'going concern'
        (c) closure.

Porter's model of competitive analysis

According to Porter there are five competitive forces which impact upon the functional strategy of any business (see Fig 1.7 opposite). These are:

1. rivalry among existing competitors
2. the threat of new entrants to the market
3. the threat of substitute products or services
4. the bargaining power of suppliers
5. the bargaining power of buyers.

A business may be evaluated using Porter's model so that its relative strengths and weaknesses can be assessed. The evaluation should consider the following factors under each heading:

1. Rivalry among existing competitors
    *   the number and size of existing competitors
    *   rate of growth
    *   product differentiation
    *   fixed and storage costs
    *   flexibility
    *   exit barriers
    *   diversity.

2. Threat of new entrants
    *   economies of scale
    *   product differentiation
    *   entry costs/other barriers
    *   access to distribution channels.

3. Threat of substitute products
    *   potential for other products or services which perform the same functions
    *   potential for other products at lower cost or better value due to technological innovation.

Fig 1.7: Porter's Model of Competitive Analysis

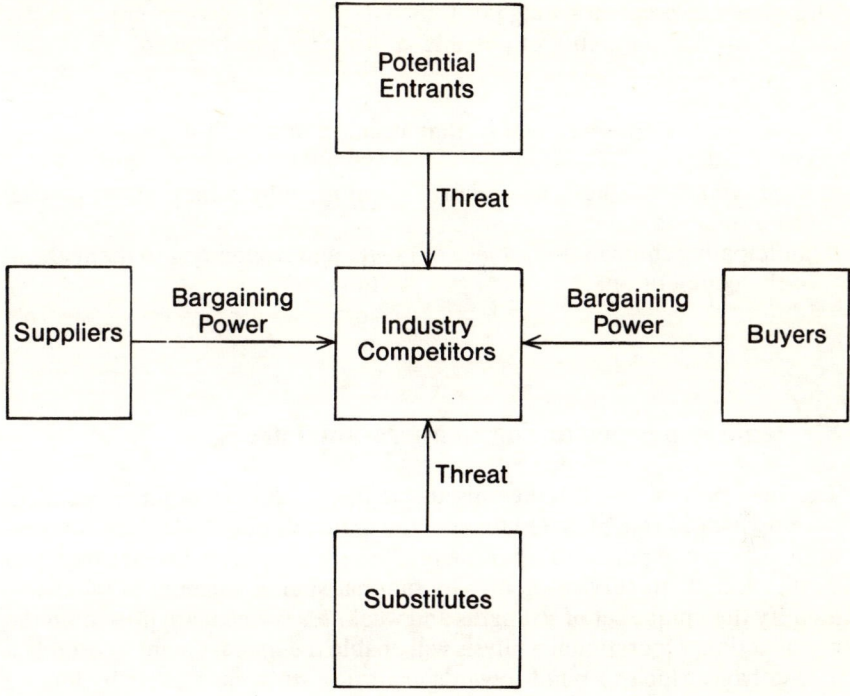

4. Supplier power
   High if:
   - more concentrated than buyers
   - buyers are not important customers
   - buyers face high switching costs
   - suppliers can vertically integrate and become competitors
   - product purchased from supplier is an important input to buyer's product.

5. Buyer power
   High if:
   - more concentrated than suppliers
   - able to purchase large volumes
   - alternative sources of supply available
   - pose threat to acquire their own source of supply (backward integration)
   - product purchased is not an important element of buyer's business.

The collective strength of the above forces driving industry competition determines the ultimate profit potential in the industry. Knowledge of these

sources of competitive pressure highlights the critical strengths and weaknesses of the business. An effective competitive strategy can then be formulated to create a strong position vis-a-vis the five competitive forces.
   This involves a number of possible approaches which include:

- positioning of the business so that strengths are built upon and threats mitigated
- improvement of the firm's relative positioning by raising brand profile/ differentiation
- anticipating shifts in the balance of power and responding to them ahead of the competition.

Strategic issues pertaining to operational areas

The first part of this chapter discussed the strategic analysis needed to develop a corporate plan and to meet the demands of industry and competition. These competitive requirements, in turn, require a broad range and depth of skills to service them. Operational skill assessment is critical to identify the unique set of strengths and weaknesses which are present in the organisation. Operational analysis will enable the management to establish a base from which to build towards achieving strategic success by linking present day strengths and weaknesses with longer term opportunities and threats.
   The constituent parts of operational analysis are shown in Fig 1.8 opposite. Operational considerations are discussed in more detail in later chapters. It is pertinent here to outline the influencing features upon the development of the strategies in each operational function.

Operational function	*Relevant strategic issues*
Marketing, Research and Development	• market positioning • marketing mix • timing • product positioning • market entry.
Production	• capacity utilisation • production processes • location of plant • equipment and maintenance.
Human Resources	• recruitment • remuneration • retention • quality/training.

Finance

- gearing/structure
- control
- funding requirements
- fund raising.

Fig 1.8: Operational Analysis

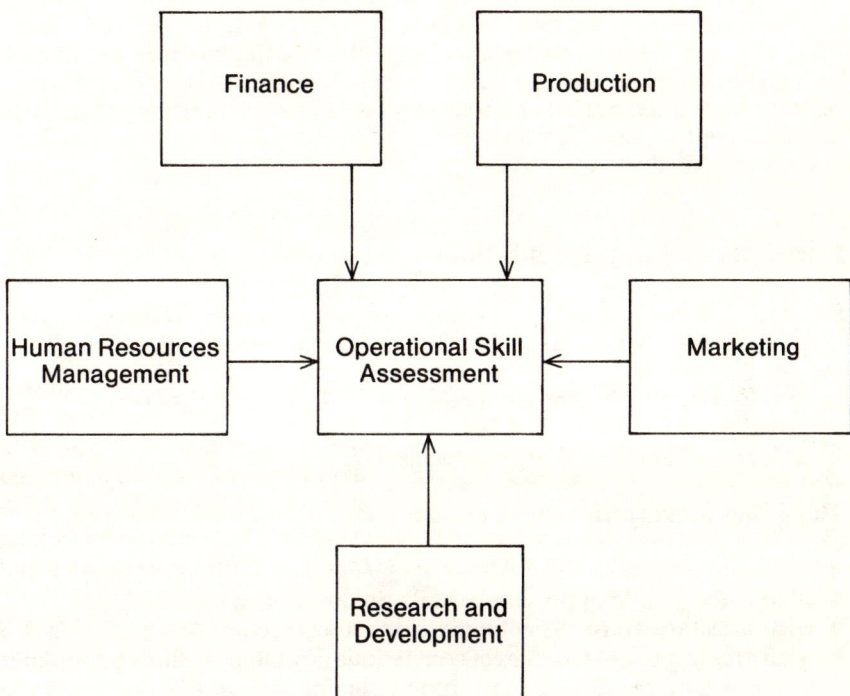

SWOT Analysis

Having carried out competitive and operational analyses, the company should be in a position to identify its strengths, weaknesses, opportunities and threats (SWOT analysis).

Strengths are positive internal abilities and situations that might enable the organisation to take a strategic advantage in achieving its objectives.
Weaknesses are internal factors and situations that might result in, or have resulted in, the organisation's failure to achieve its objectives.
Opportunities are favourable external factors and situations that will assist the organisation in achieving its objectives.
Threats are unfavourable characteristics in the company's long-term operating environment.

The purpose of a SWOT analysis is two-fold:

1. it will help management to assess just how difficult the achievement of particular goals will be, and

2. it should highlight key competitive advantages and disadvantages and seek to match these unique features to the organisation's goals.

The first step is to identify the internal strengths and weaknesses of the company and then identify the external opportunities and threats as perceived by management.

The second step is to assess the likely impact of each strength and weakness upon the opportunities and threats identified.

This assessment is necessarily subjective and qualitative and will range from 'very positive' to 'very negative' impact. Once this has been performed the management should have a clear perception of which opportunities can be exploited easily and which threats are most serious. A strategy can then be developed around this analysis to build upon existing strengths and assuage potential threats.

Decisions and implementation

Strategic thinking is about asking (and attempting to answer) questions. The essence of strategy may be summed up in two simple questions:

1. what is, or could be, my competitive advantage in terms of cost or value (price)?
2. why and where is that advantage sustainable?

These questions in turn require one to answer a host of other questions, such as:

- what is the profile of my competitors, in terms of cost and value?
- what is the structure of my industry or market sector?
- what are the possible sources of competitive advantage within that sector?
- how much potential does it afford for sustainable profits?
- how much opportunity is there to build a competitive advantage through focusing on a specific market segment?

Strategy, however, must be translated into decisions and actions. Taking strategic decisions requires the company to make a conscious choice of attractive markets (in terms of sustainable profit potential) and the means by which it will achieve a competitive advantage within them. It then requires commitment and concentration of the requisite resources (managerial, financial and other) to achieve that advantage. Many strategies fail because management will not choose from the alternatives and/or will not concentrate resources in the areas that are of importance. Half-heartedness will not win.

Since a business is often a collection of functional activities, held together by the overall strategy, effective implementation of the strategy requires that the company pursues a consistent, co-ordinated and explicit set of actions. The actions must be:

- consistent, because they must relate to each other and form an integrated plan
- co-ordinated, because they must be taken in the right time relationship to each other

- explicit, because managers must understand what they are doing, why they are doing it, and how it relates to the whole.

These requirements ensure that effective strategy formulation has to involve participation and communication. Both of these are areas where the growing business often fails. Generally speaking, the degree to which the strategy, or strategic plan, should be documented, varies from business to business. There can be little doubt that, in all but the smallest company, details must be documented for the purposes of dissemination and communication. This does not, however, justify the dead weight of paper-driven strategic planning processes which hinder many large companies.

As a first step in the implementation of its strategic decisions, the growing business should document in a structured, clear and concise manner its objectives and plans for achievement of those objectives within a formal 'Business Plan'.

The business plan

All growing businesses should have a business plan. The business plan is an essential management tool. The plan should explain where the business is currently placed; where it intends to go and how it is to get there. It can be used as a budget against which to monitor present and future performance and it will assist in identifying potential problem areas so that prompt corrective action may be taken. Moreover, the format can be easily adapted, and content expanded, so that the plan can be used as a medium for a fund raising proposal.

The advantages of preparing a business plan may be summarised as follows:

- a company's objectives can be formalised and the practical steps by which those objectives are to be achieved can be established and communicated to both management and employees
- the financial implications of initiating plans can be projected. If a funding requirement is identified, the plan can be used by financiers to assist in their assessment of the potential of the business
- the company has a standard against which it can objectively measure its performance to date
- members of the management team can be assessed against performance targets, thus assisting in the motivation and monitoring of staff
- potential problems should be identified at an earlier stage than would otherwise be the case and action can be initiated to reduce their impact.

The amount of detail required in the plan will depend largely upon the final purpose of the document and the knowledge of the business which the intended user possesses. A prospective third party investor will usually require a comprehensive plan, to include a review of past trading and detailed CVs of the management team. Similarly, if the plan is being prepared by a subsidiary for its holding company in a group where that subsidiary operates quite independently, outside the main group activities, then the detailed requirements may be as demanding as those for a third party user. Conversely, the level of detail on past results and management required by the owner/managers of a smaller business, using the plan as an internal document only, will be minimal.

The structure of a typical business plan is outlined below and it assumes that the plan is to be used as a medium for a fund raising proposal. Consequently the amount of detail on past results and the management team can be reduced if the plan is to be used for internal purposes only.

Structure of the plan

The basic structure of the plan should be organised under the following headings:

1. introduction/executive summary
2. operations/products/services
3. market/competition
4. management
5. past trading
6. future trading
7. funding requirements
8. appendices.

Consideration is now given to the information which could be included under each of the above sections.

INTRODUCTION/EXECUTIVE SUMMARY

The first step before commencing the plan is to decide what the objectives of the business are, in both financial and qualitative terms. The objectives should be determined by the needs of the owners, management team, financiers, customers and employees. There may be conflicting objectives held by each of these interested parties but clearly those of the proprietors should take priority in determining the overall business objectives. A key to successful business management is to co-ordinate the varying goals of interested parties so that they are complementary to the overall business objectives, this is the concept of 'goal congruence'. The simplest illustration of this is where the business objective is to maximise profits whilst the employees' objective is normally to maximise personal income. Management could make these potentially conflicting objectives complementary by introducing a performance related pay scheme for employees, linked to profit generation. Such a scheme cannot be implemented in isolation but may be one element of the business planning process.

Once the key objectives have been set, many companies will encapsulate these within a 'mission statement'. The mission statement essentially gives the company a focus for its objectives so that all strategic decisions are made with these goals in mind. The objectives of the company, or mission statement, should be stated in the introduction to the business plan.

The introduction should be as brief as possible but must convey concisely and clearly the unique factors that are relevant to the business and that will help it achieve its objectives. In practice this is often one of the most difficult sections of the plan to construct.

If the plan is to be used in a fund raising proposal the introduction should also outline the nature of the business, its background and provide a brief product description. In addition, a brief resume of the management team should be provided along with some financial data. The introduction can be limited to a summary table of key financial data which should include historic and forecast turnover and profits and must quantify any funding requirement, giving the purpose of the requirement. It may also be appropriate to summarise the current capital structure and funding package within this section.

Finally, the introduction should detail a timetable of future key events. For instance, the anticipated date of a new product launch, the timing of new funding, the opening of a new outlet or manufacturing facility, the operational date for new machinery, the recruitment of personnel, and so on.

OPERATIONS/PRODUCTS/SERVICES

This section of the plan should begin with an outline history of the business since its formation, with increased emphasis given to the most recent period of operations.

Each product or services of the business should be described. In addition, proposed new products should be introduced. The product descriptions should highlight any unique features and the benefits of the products to the customers or to the business itself (for instance where commonality of components makes it possible to switch production from one product to another).

The production process for a manufacturing concern or the modus operandi for a service company should be described. Diagrams or flowcharts may be employed here to illustrate how the business operates. This exercise may highlight any weaknesses in the operations, such as production bottlenecks or shortages in the resources required to produce the products or services.

Consideration should also be given to any research and development requirements as well as government or other regulations covering operations.

Finally, existing resources of the business (premises, personnel, plant and machinery) should be described and any future requirements which may result from expansion should be noted.

MARKET/COMPETITION

Under this heading management should take the opportunity to identify the target market. Existing and new markets should be distinguished and barriers to entry considered. Management should consider deterents to new players entering their market as well as the obstacles they themselves will face when entering a new market sector. Porter's model of competitive analysis may usefully be employed here.

The key findings of any market research should be summarised within this section. An attempt should be made to quantify the present and future market size, along with the company's present and anticipated market share. An action plan should be formulated to demonstrate how the business is to achieve the anticipated increase in market share. The action plan will clearly have to take into account the findings of the market research and should attempt to exploit any opportunities and address any weaknesses revealed by the research.

A review of the market should include an identification of the company's major customers, both actual and prospective, and thus may reveal an over dependence on a limited customer base. In this event, management may need to develop a growth strategy built upon gaining new customers rather than just developing existing ones.

Competitors should also be considered and an assessment made to provide an indication of the company's relative strengths and weaknesses. The company and its competitors should be compared so as to highlight differences in pricing policy, market positioning, market share and historic performance. It would also be appropriate to consider the relative strategies and objectives of the company and its competitors.

Consideration should also be given to sales and distribution practices and the level of advertising and public relations activity that is needed to support the continuing growth of the business.

MANAGEMENT

This section should be based on an organisational structure which may be illustrated by an organigram representation of the levels of authority and responsibilities of the various personnel. The structure should show the reporting lines and identify, by name and title, the key members of the management team.

If the plan is to be used by a third party it should include a section on each member of the team giving details of:

- age
- key responsibilities
- experience/qualifications
- significant accomplishments.

The section should comment on how the individual talents of the management team will contribute to the company's future development. This exercise may identify weaknesses in the present team and any critical skills lacking. Eventually, all growing businesses should strive to develop a management team who possess, between them, the organisational, technical, financial, marketing and sales skills necessary to support the level of growth to which the business aspires. Management must be satisfied that the business possesses the necessary personnel resources to achieve the stated objectives of the company.

If a particular skill gap has been identified by this process, the plan should address how this weakness is to be resolved. Obviously, the most straight forward option may be recruitment. This may, however, be expensive and because of this it is common for growing businesses to rely upon external consultants such as accountants or marketing specialists, at least in the early stages of development. Alternatively, skill shortages may be addressed by providing suitable training for existing personnel.

PAST TRADING

Under this heading, a summary of the financial results for the past three to five years should be presented. The figures should be taken from both the statutory and latest management accounts.

These figures should also be accompanied by a review of the historic profit and loss accounts on a line by line basis (sales, gross profit, overheads and net profit) so as to identify:

- milestones
- trends
- extraordinary income/expenditure
- reasons for losses/down-turn in growth etc.

In addition, a review of the latest balance sheet should be undertaken together with a comparison of recent cash/overdraft movements against available bank facilities.

FUTURE TRADING

This section should begin with a summary of the profit projections for the foreseeable period, which may be up to five years. The detailed projections should include integrated profit and loss accounts, cashflow forecasts and balance sheets and should also be accompanied by a schedule of the assumptions inherent in the forecasts.

The main issue to be addressed in this section is the justification of these assumptions.

The forecast results should be compared to:

- historic results
- industry averages
- competitors' results
- current order book/potential sales identified.

Any major discrepancies between the forecast results and the above items will need to be explained.

In addition, the sales forecasts should be given substance by the research included in the marketing section of the plan. Indeed, it is imperative that a link is established between this section and all other sections of the plan as stated strategies will obviously impact upon future financial results.

To the income and expense assumptions should be added receipt and payment assumptions and capital expenditure assumptions. In this way a cashflow forecast for the period can be formulated and balance sheets produced.

A review of these cashflow assumptions should also be made in order to justify the forecasts.

Any funding requirement will be highlighted by the cashflow forecast, the amount and timing of which should be stated in this section.

The next step is to identify those risks revealed during the review of the forecasts and attempt to assess their impact upon the projections by changing the relevant assumption in isolation and recording its impact upon the forecast results—both in terms of profit and funding requirements. This process is known as Sensitivity Analysis and is a useful tool in assessing the risks associated with a failure to achieve forecast results. The analysis should identify the major risks within the projections. Once this has been done management should consider a contingency plan of action to be taken should a key sensitivity impact on the projected results.

The appropriate action will clearly depend upon the nature of the shortfall. However, management must ask 'if this slippage occurs, what corrective course of action is available to the company?'

FUNDING REQUIREMENTS

This section may not be applicable if funding is not required. Otherwise it should give the level and timing of funding requirements, including any buffer which may have been built into the requirement to cover potential shortfalls as identified in the sensitivity analysis.

Investment in the company from existing or potential shareholders and managers should be quantified, along with other potential sources of funds identified.

APPENDICES

The following items may be included within the appendices:

- product brochures/photographs/drawings
- market research report
- CVs of management/organisation chart
- historic accounts
- five year financial projections and assumptions
  —profit and loss accounts
  —cashflow
  —balance sheets
    the first two or three years should be done on a monthly basis, annual projections will normally suffice thereafter
  —sensitivity analyses.

Some general tips on the preparation of the plan

1. the appropriate length of the business plan will usually depend upon the level and type of funding required and the complexity of the business. Typically, however, business plans run from 15 to 50 pages in length, excluding appendices
2. include a contents page, number each paragraph and, if the plan is very long, include cross-referencing where appropriate
3. prepare the summary/introduction as a last step. This section should appear at the beginning and, if the plan is being used to raise finance, must be of sufficient quality to ensure the reader has a desire to read the whole document; this can, accordingly, be the most important part of the plan. You should remember to inform the reader of the level of funding required in this section
4. do not include excessive jargon. Keep the description of products/services simple and express in layman's terms—relegate technical details to an appendix
5. summarise and simplify in the main body of the plan—relegate as much detail as possible to appendices
6. include the latest statutory and management accounts figures

7. attempt to justify all key assumptions used in the projections
8. identify any weaknesses that are apparent to you, and attempt to address these within the plan. Do not try to hide weaknesses
9. seek advice from your accountant on the detailed contents of the plan and ask him to review it before it is finalised
10. if prepared properly, the business plan will be a useful tool for management in focusing their efforts towards the company's key objectives. It is important, therefore, that sufficient time and effort is taken in preparing the plan so as correctly to identify the key objectives and the manner in which these can be achieved
11. the plan should be co-ordinated by the person who effectively manages the business. The senior management team as a whole must also be involved in the preparation of the plan, as they should be able to provide useful input to the strategic issues which must be addressed if the business is to succeed
12. if a plan is to be a useful management tool, it must not be seen as a static document. It is likely that management's objectives will change over time and it is important that these changes are reflected in an updated plan.

Of equal importance, is the monitoring of actual results by comparison to those projected in the document, whether these be financial or otherwise (eg the perception of the company in the market, quality control standards etc). Deviations from the plan should be analysed and reasons identified. Amendments to the corporate plan may then need to be made to reflect this past experience.

Some issues affecting strategy for the growing business

So far, a substantial part of our analysis applies as equally to larger businesses as to smaller businesses. What might distinguish the nature of strategy or the process of strategy development in a growing business? The answer could be one of several things, which in broad terms can be classified under three main headings—Objectives, Organisation and Finance. Under the first heading, comes the personal objectives of the founder/entrepreneur and the financial objectives of the shareholder (who may be one and the same person). Under the second heading comes the role and involvement of the entrepreneur in the business, the relative position of his subordinates, and the need for improved communications. The third heading covers accessibility to, and expertise in, finance.

Objectives

Since the entrepreneur or founder will in most cases be the 'raison d'etre' of the company, his personal objectives become significant influences (and potentially constraints) on the development of the strategy. Why did he establish the business; was it to pursue technological excellence, was it because he had a good idea, is he out to win the 'game', is he after growth or comfort?

As well as personal objectives, entrepreneurs usually have financial objectives. If there are other shareholders, they will certainly have financial objectives. All shareholders look for a return on their investment; the question is—when do they want it? Are they looking for financial security and a rapid payback, thereby necessitating heavy dividend payments and a diminution of retained profit for reinvestment? Or are they happy to defer their return for the time being on the promise of a capital gain at a later date and leave profits in the business for reinvestment? These concerns are more acute for the smaller, growing business where shareholders are few in number and less homogeneous than for the larger and quoted entity. They become even more acute, of course, in the event that the various share-holders do not have similar requirements for income and are unable to agree on a financial policy. Potentially, therefore, shareholders' financial objec-tives are a significant influence on the development of the business.

Organisation

These issues tend to arise as the entrepreneur continues to react as if the business were still small. He will probably not have considered it worthwhile to develop a formal strategy or business definition in the formative years, even though he may have a well formed mental idea of his objectives. This is despite the fact that he may well have prepared a short 'Business Plan' to obtain start-up finance. The problems arise because, as the business grows, the entrepreneur's span of control broadens and he becomes more remote from the source of business decisions. However, at the same time, he cannot get away from the notion that strategy is a 'back of the envelope' subject and fails to recognise that more people need to know what is intended in the short, medium and long term. This tension between the need to make strategy more explicit, and the desire to keep it implicit, may well continue up to a public flotation when the requirement for an explicit business plan embodying statements of strategy is externally imposed. The earlier in the life of the business that the entrepreneur can involve his colleagues and staff in the development of strategy, the more effective will be the ensuing course of action.

Even if the entrepreneur does succeed in 'breaking out' and involving his managers more, there is a possibility that the past failure to release his control will have resulted in subordinates whose authority to carry out the required actions has been undefined, or in subordinates with limited skills.

A final issue related to organisation concerns resources. Strategic think-ing requires time and information. Both may be a precious resource in the growing business, and the latitude to increase either of them difficult to improve. Nevertheless, efforts must be made to improve this situation in the interests of improved strategic decision making.

Finance

The sources of finance for the growing company may be relatively limited, especially debt finance. This clearly has a major impact on the range of alternative strategies that a growing business can consider. In addition, such businesses are often characterised, historically, by a lack of financial expertise in the management team, which compounds the problem of non-accessibility to funds.

These are no more than a selection of factors which can impact upon the strategy of a growing business. In general, they do not alter the need to seek a competitive advantage in attractive markets. What they can affect is the ability to look at a full range of alternatives, to select the strategy most appropriate to the long-term health of the business, or to put the strategy into action in an effective fashion.

Conclusion

As was stressed early in this chapter, each situation is unique in strategic terms and no universal prescription for strategy development is available. However, it is possible to produce a framework within which one asks the right questions to establish the facts upon which the strategy can be based.

Such a framework might appear as detailed in Fig 1.9:

Fig 1.9: A Framework for the Development of a Corporate Plan

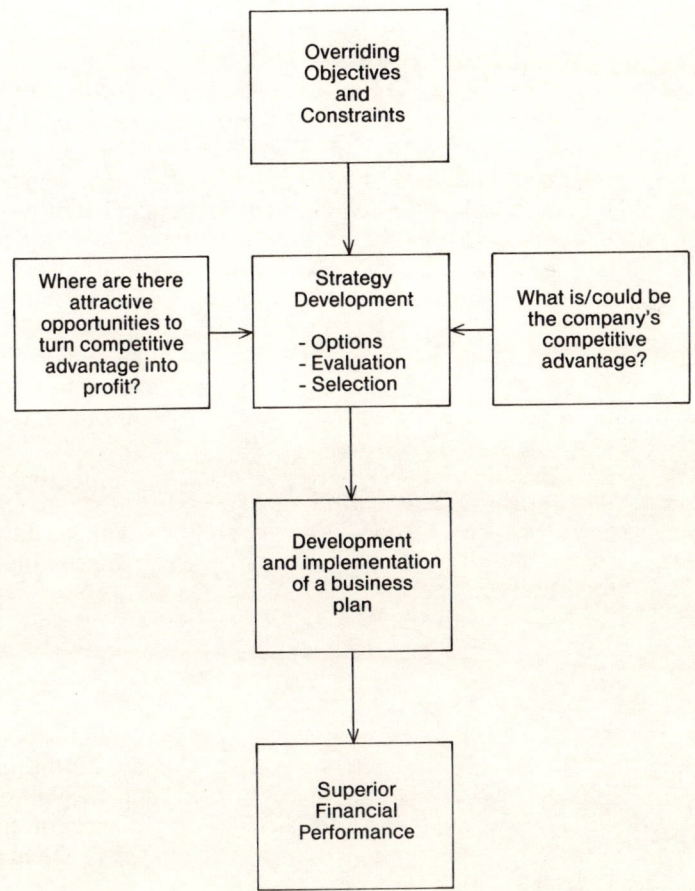

Throughout, this book will stress the importance of adequate planning, whether it is with regard to the implementation of a new computer system (Chapter 2), or the development of an acquisitions strategy (Chapter 8). It is perhaps not surprising therefore that this chapter on corporate planning is the linchpin in the management of corporate growth.

Chapter 2 discusses the information systems required to monitor the financial performance of the company and Chapters 5, 6 and 7 review the marketing, operational and human resource issues that the company should consider when formulating its plans. Before these, however, Chapter 3 gives some consideration to the issues which will be of interest to a potential financier when making an assessment of a business and its plans for growth.

CHAPTER 2

Management Information Systems

Introduction

Any business, but in particular the growing business, will encounter a scarcity of resources at critical stages in its evolution. These scarce resources will typically include personnel, machinery, materials, or finance. Accordingly, the management of a growing business must allocate available resources in a manner which enables the company to achieve the corporate objectives as identified in the company business plan. It is clear, therefore, that a scarcity of resources and the need to achieve objectives lead to a need for decision making. It is also obvious that, when taking a decision on resource allocation, management cannot be certain that the impact of their decisions will necessarily satisfy the corporate objectives. Management will, however, be able to look to various sources of information such as market research, historic results, competitors' performance, costings and pricings etc, to assist in taking final decisions. This is why information is crucial—quite simply it enables management to make decisions based on facts.

The fundamental rule in assessing whether information is relevant is that it should ultimately improve management's forecasts of the outcome of future events following on from specific courses of action. The network of related procedures developed to collect data and translate this into *relevant* information is often referred to as 'The Management Information System' and is the subject matter for this chapter.

The chapter will begin with an explanation of Systems Analysis. This is the process of identifying management's information requirements in order to establish specific objectives and design specifications for an information system. The chapter will then discuss the Accounting Information System as this is frequently the most pervasive and largest of the management information sub-systems in a commercial organisation.

The Accounting Information System is itself often comprised of several sub-systems, such as:

- sales and credit control
- purchases and payments
- production and cost control
- timekeeping and payroll.

This chapter will also concentrate on one of these components, namely the costing system, as this is often a key element in the setting of economic pricing and cost controls as well as playing a key role in aiding an understanding of how resources may be utilised in the growing company. There is an obvious inter-relationship between the market for a product, the costs associated with production, and the final price achieved. This link, between costing information and pricing information, is explored further before providing examples of the type of information demanded by a pricing system.

Typically, in a growing business the market will demand a fast and flexible response to change, not only so that any necessary pricing adjustments may be made speedily, but also so that decisions with regard to production, marketing, human resources and other operational areas can be made as soon as new relevant information becomes available.

As a consequence, the information systems of growing businesses should function in the most efficient manner possible, given the scale of current operations as well as considering future requirements. The managers of these companies encounter many similar problems in managing their operations as do large publicly-owned businesses in so far as information needs are concerned. To handle the increasing variety and complexity of the situations facing the growing company, the systems must provide useful information on a timely basis. If the present system does not satisfy this test, management must consider amending the systems to produce the information required for fully effective management.

There are two principal factors which create the need for change in the information systems of a business. These are firstly, the actual growth in the business itself and secondly, improvements in information technology which may provide competitive advantage. These factors may lead management to consider adopting a computerised system (or upgrading the existing system). The final part of this chapter will review the advantages and disadvantages of computerisation before giving some guidance on the implementation of such a system.

Systems analysis

Systems analysis is the process of identifying management's information requirements in order to establish objectives and specifications for an information system, as the first step in the development or improvement of the system.

The information needs of management

An assessment of management's information needs should commence with the identification of the decisions that management needs to make, which in turn will indicate the information that is required. A framework for the identification of management decisions is provided by Anthony (R N Anthony, *Planning & Control Systems, A Framework for Analysis*, 1986, Harvard University Press) who categorises management functions into three areas as illustrated in Fig 2.1 opposite.

The responsibility for these three functional areas are in turn apportioned between top, middle and lower management with some overlaps (see Fig 2.2 on page 32).

It follows that the type of information required by a manager is dependent upon his level in the organisation. Lower management information needs should be relatively straightforward to satisfy since most of this information

Fig 2.1: Anthony's Classification of Management Functions

Strategic Planning	Management	Operational Control
Choosing company objectives	Formulating budgets	Implementing policies
Planning the organisation	Planning staff levels	Controlling hiring
Setting financial policies	Working capital planning	Controlling credit extension
Setting marketing policies	Formulating advertising programmes	Controlling placement of advertisements
Setting research policies	Deciding on research projects	
Choosing new product lines	Choosing product improvements	
Acquiring a new division	Deciding on plant rearrangement	Scheduling production
Deciding on non-routine capital expenditure	Deciding on routine capital expenditure	
Setting personnel policies	Formulating decision rules for operational control	Controlling inventory
	Measuring, appraising, and improving management performance	Measuring, appraising, and improving workers' efficiency

can be obtained from sources which are internal to the organisation. Top level management needs are much more difficult to identify because the functions of strategic planning are very broadly defined, volatile and future orientated. Their needs are difficult to satisfy because the information requirements are primarily external. The information required for management control is, in the main, sourced from within the organisation, is based on narrow time horizons, is needed on a relatively frequent and timely basis, and must above all be accurate.

Objectives of the information system

Once the information needs of management have been identified with the help of Anthony's framework, the specific objectives of the information system can be determined. Some general objectives for information systems are given in Cushings, *Accounting Information Systems and Business Organisations* (1978, 2nd edition, Addison-Wesley Publishing) and are reproduced on page 32:

Fig 2.2: The Relationship of Decision Categories to Management Levels

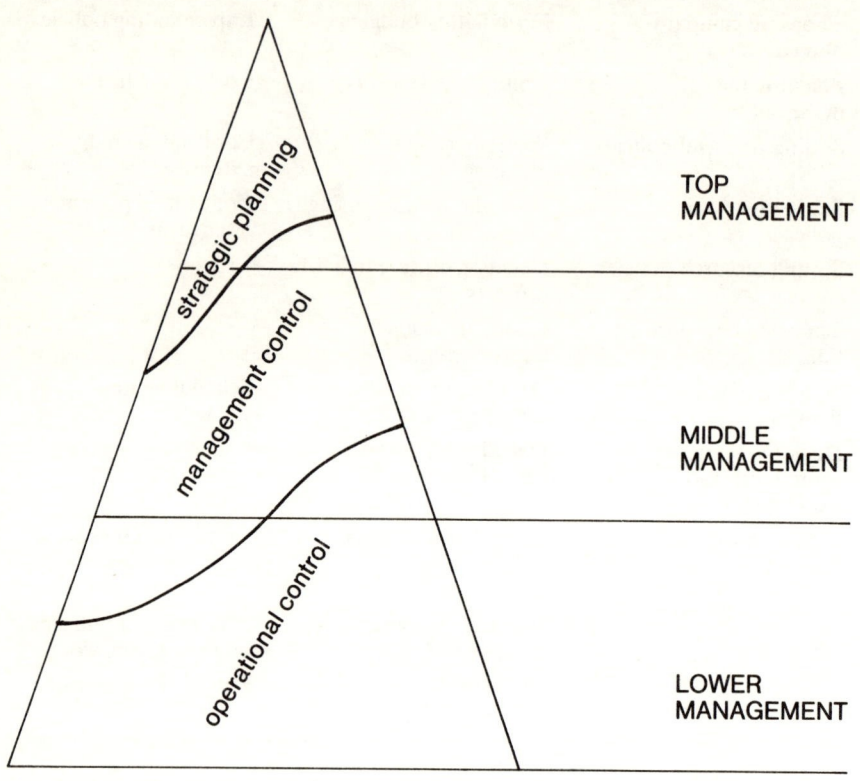

1. *usefulness*   The system should produce information which is timely and relevant for decision making by management and operating personnel within the organisation
2. *economy*   All component parts of the system, including reports, controls, machines, etc, should contribute a benefit value at least as great as their cost
3. *reliability*   System output should possess a high degree of accuracy, and the system itself should be capable of operating effectively even while a human component is absent or while a machine component is temporarily inoperative
4. *customer service*   The system should provide courteous and efficient customer service at points of interface with the organisation's customers
5. *capacity*   The system should have sufficient capacity to handle periods of peak operation as well as periods of normal capacity
6. *simplicity*   The system should be simple enough that its structure and operations can be easily understood and its procedures easily accomplished
7. *flexibility*   The system should be sufficiently flexible to accommodate changes of a reasonable magnitude in the conditions under which it operates or in the requirements imposed upon it by the organisation.

Systems survey

The specification of the information system can be detailed once the needs and objectives of the system are known. The first stage in this process is to document the present system and highlight any weaknesses, where the needs and objectives are not being satisfied. The investigation of the present system will focus upon three key areas:

1. resources—personnel, computer hardware and software
2. information and data, input, output, files and documentation
3. procedures and functions.

The review carried out will comprise the systems survey which may indicate the need to amend the present system in some way.

There are two principal factors which create the need for change in the information systems of a business:

- the growth of the business, leading to different types of information needs and a greater volume of data processing
- improvements in information technology which can provide competitive advantages to those companies who are in the vanguard of innovation.

Both of these factors can lead the company to consider adopting a computerised system (or upgrading the existing computer system). 'The computer decision' is discussed later in this chapter.

The following section will concentrate upon the functions and characteristics of the Accounting Information System, as this is often the largest of the management information sub-systems.

Accounting information system

The accounting information system can be described, in addition to any statutory or fiscal requirements, as the means through which the management of a company can understand, plan and control the operations of the business. The accounting system is the circulatory tract for the business transactions which permit the organisation to function.

To speak of an accounting 'system' implies that the management of a growing business order their jobs to enable them to cope with the many complex problems within the operating environment. This ordering of the environment is done through the establishment of procedures. 'System' and 'procedure' may be differentiated as follows:

A system is a network of related procedures developed according to one integrated scheme for performing a major activity of the business.

A procedure is a sequence of clerical operations, usually involving several people in one or more departments, established to ensure uniform handling of a recurring transaction of the business.

The accounting system, through its network of related procedures, provides a structure to receive input, process the input, create output, allow feedback and control the operation.

The functioning of this network enables the managers of growing businesses:

- *to determine the results of operations*   This function involves: (a) in systems terms, *distribution* (ie abstracting quantity and financial information from business documents) and (b) the production of reports for management
- *to monitor the assets and liabilities of the business*   This function involves keeping financial accounts for cash, accounts with customers, accounts with suppliers, accounts for plant and equipment, accounts with proprietors, and so forth
- *to get things done*   To purchase materials or goods for resale, to instruct the factory to produce, to instruct the warehouse employees to fill orders and the shipping clerks to ship them, and so forth. In this connection, the various order procedures in a business are of relevance
- *to facilitate planning of business activities, follow-up of performance, and adjustment of plans*   Thus, (a) production planning and production order procedures are initiated to inform the factory of production values required and the timetable, (b) actual production is compared with planned production and (c) adjusted production schedules made in the light of current and expected factory performance, stock levels, unfilled customers' orders and expected sales.

The accounting system is not an abstraction or a concept, but rather, a collator and processor of data which management can then translate into useful information for the achievement of stated goals.

Accounting systems function within a company environment. The environment affects the accounting system since it encompasses the goals, needs, activities and individuals of the organisation that are utilising the system. Conversely, the accounting system's ability to generate data to meet the requirements of these elements impacts upon the environment.

The accounting system interacts with its environment as input and output cross the system. There are two main types of input: input to be acted on by the system to generate output, and input which improves and controls the system. Output is produced from the actions of the system components upon the input. This input is often fed back to the system to check the processes taking place within the system. The regulation of activities and processes is illustrated in Fig 2.3 opposite. This interaction of the system with its environment enables management to control operations so that the basic objectives of the business are achieved.

The accounting system as a whole includes the full spectrum of forms, papers, journals, ledgers and financial and operating statements used to record and accumulate data. Each accounting system consists of several interrelated sub-systems. An improved understanding of a system as a whole may be obtained by examining its sub-systems. These components or sub-systems comprising the accounting system may include:

- sales and credit control
- purchases and payments
- production and cost control
- timekeeping and payroll.

Fig 2.3: Basics of an Accounting System

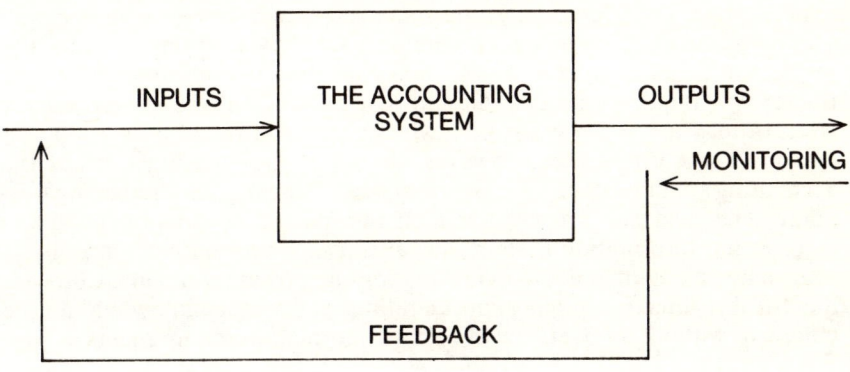

These sub-systems must be moulded to the needs of the business that they serve so that the information provided is up-to-date, comprehensive and meaningful. For this to be possible, the activities associated with each sub-system must be delineated. These activities are as follows:

SALES AND CASH
CREDIT CONTROL

Order entry
Sales and shipping orders
Invoicing
Inventory control
Sales distribution
Accounts receivable
Cash receipts
Credit control

PURCHASES AND
PAYMENTS

Purchase orders
Receiving reports
Expense distribution
Vouchers payable
Accounts payable
Cash disbursements

PRODUCTION
AND COST CONTROL

Production orders
Inventory control
Cost accounting

TIMEKEEPING
AND PAYROLL

Employment records
Timekeeping
Labour distribution

These activities create the input for the accounting system. Not every growing company would require all these activities, and therefore, the sub-systems amongst companies will differ. The particular activities undertaken will affect both the quality and quantity of output produced by the various systems. Additionally, the same sub-system in one company will vary substantially from that of another because of the differing nature of the services or products arising. Both a manufacturing organisation and a contractor will require a production and cost system, but the manufacturing concern may use a process system whereas the contractor uses a job cost system. These differences, however, do not change the functions of the accounting system, which will remain constant from organisation to organisation. The next section will focus on one particular component of the Accounting Information System, namely costing information, since this is often a key element in decision making for the growing company. Costs are inextricably linked to pricing considerations and this section would not be complete without an overview of pricing information requirements.

Costing information

What is a costing system?

It is a system that can readily identify the costs, associated with all or some of the following for a specified time period:

- a function or responsibility area, eg marketing
- a process, say manufacture or distribution
- a geographical area
- a customer
- a product.

A costing system assists in decision making, the setting of realistic targets and the understanding of how resources will be utilised in the growing company. The application of related statistical techniques to the cost information further strengthens the ability of the company to manage growth by increasing the accuracy of future plans.

Classification of costs

Costs may be historical, forecast or standard. They can be identified as variable, or semi-variable within a given volume. Some costs are often classified as fixed (eg rent) although in the long run most costs are ultimately variable (ie new premises can be found etc).

The level of detail required will vary according to factors such as the industry, size of product range, number of customers etc. A manufacturing company may focus on material costs with a costing system that details the breakdown of such costs. A retail organisation may wish to focus on a detailed analysis of labour, or stockholding and distribution costs.

Product customer costing

It is often in the area of product or customer costing that growing companies need to focus attention. Here labour, material and overhead costs are identified with individual product lines or customers. Traditional methods of allocating overheads on the basis of production volume or sales, are often now superseded by methods that identify the causes (or drivers) of costs. For example, the number of parts in a product, or the number of outlets for a particular customer, the delivery size for distribution costs etc.

Scarce resource

The costing system may detail the quantity of scarce resource utilised in the production of each product (category) so as to enable the calculation of the contribution per unit of scarce resource consumed. If there is more than one scarce resource then statistical linear programming techniques will be required to determine the optimal product mix.

In the context of managing growth, the relevant cost information is the incremental cost of future growth—be it through increasing the product range or expanding output capability. Historic costs are largely irrelevant in decision making, except to the extent that the historic costs will assist management to predict likely future costs.

Moreover, in a situation where the company faces a scarcity of resources, the cost of a product (or a particular activity) should include the foregone contribution of the most profitable alternative product which the company could have produced with that scarce resource. This is the 'opportunity cost' concept.

A major High Street retailer, which owns most of its shop premises, has recognised this concept and, as a consequence, its internal shop budgets include a charge, in each store's profit and loss account, equivalent to an economic market rent for the premises occupied by the shop. Target profits given to store managers are accordingly more demanding because sales now need to cover the opportunity cost of the scarce resource used.

Linking costing to pricing—feed-forward approach

There is an inter-relationship between the market for the product or service, the costs, and the final sales price (see Fig 2.4 on page 38). A costing system forms an integral part of this process by guiding the design, manufacturing and purchasing elements of the inter-relationship to achieve required margins in a dynamic market.

Pricing information

Pricing decisions are often complex and some of the financial information necessary to make such decisions will be provided by the costing system. In many multi-product, multi-market companies pricing is not simply a matter of setting figures at which the company's products are offered to customers. Selling price is one of a number of variables in the marketing mix. There are many others, for example, competition, quality, customer service, and delivery lead times.

**Fig 2.4: The Feed-Forward System of Planning
and Control of Costs**

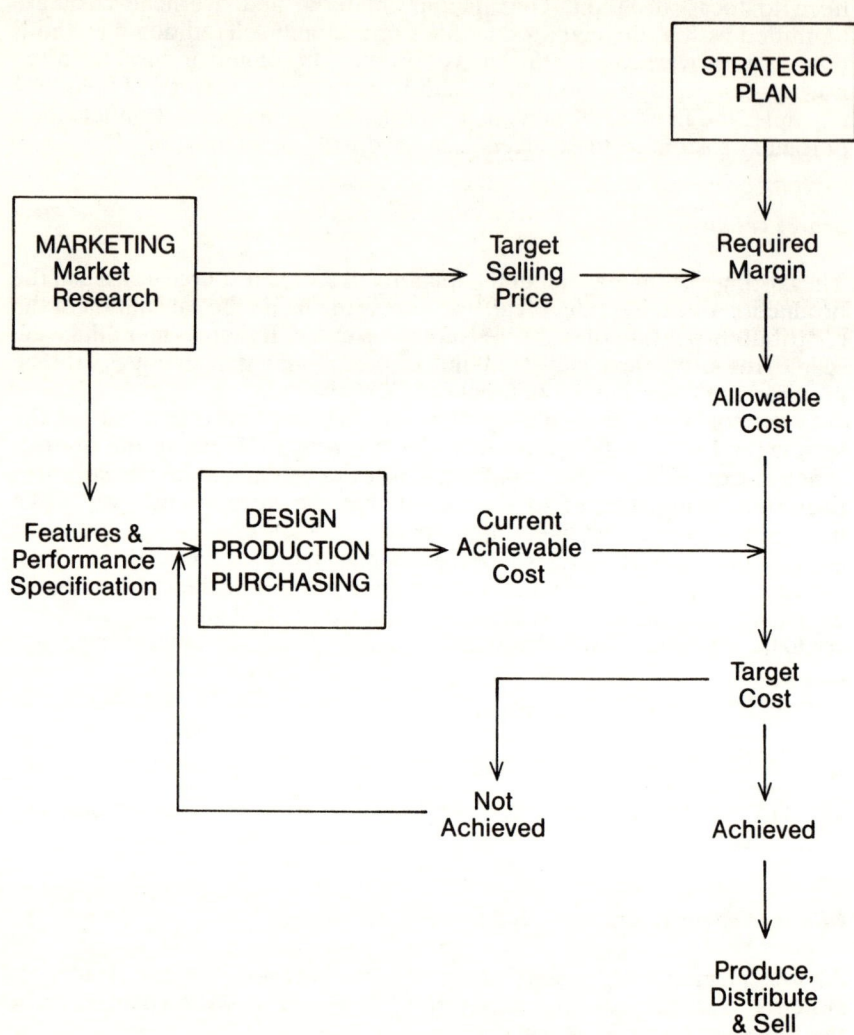

Cost plus pricing

The company's costing system should provide an economic price that the company could charge for each product—this will be equivalent to the incremental cost of that product. A price set below this level would result in a negative contribution in the short term. The implication is that prices should be set at a level above this cost such that fixed costs are covered and a 'reasonable' overall profit achieved—a 'cost plus' approach. However, ultimately, there are many other factors influencing pricing decisions which render a cost plus based pricing policy redundant. A particular weakness with the cost plus approach is that it assumes that the cost base of the company is 'reasonable'. If the market has 'established' a price, a company may need to alter its cost structure in order to be profitable in the long term rather than just change its pricing policy.

Understanding demand

Cost-based prices are a reference point in determining selling prices but they cannot be viewed in isolation. An in-depth understanding of the demand for a product or service is the crucial factor. The price-sensitivity not only varies between products and markets, but also varies with time.

Management's knowledge of a particular market will originate from sound marketing information. Management experience and intuition may well make an important contribution to the final decision. This 'intelligence' can be supplemented by market research surveys used to assess the response of potential customers to the product at various prices. In addition, if there are currently similar products on the market, the prices charged by competitors will obviously provide a benchmark for price setting.

In the long term, the optimal price will be the one where the greatest total contribution is generated from sales. If it is a new product this may involve the use of discounts in the short term in order to establish the product in the market place.

The potential impact of advertising upon demand should not be ignored. Again this impact may be estimated from past experience or controlled experiments (such as regional advertising) supported by further market research.

Finally, it should be remembered that the ability to predict the outcome of changes in demand, and then to co-ordinate alternative courses of action, in a manner consistent with a company strategy, is dependent on sound links between the costing system, the business planning system, and the approach to pricing.

Information for monitoring

An essential first stage in any pricing decision is a comprehensive monitoring system that signals the need for a price review. Such a system would collect the following types of information:

1. sales, in units and value:
   - previous year comparisons
   - different markets/channels comparisons
   - budget v actual comparisons
   - forecast v actual comparisons
   - forecast v budget comparisons
   - target v actual comparisons
2. competitors' prices and conditions of sale
3. inquiries from potential customers about a product
4. sales at 'below list' prices:
   - measured as a percentage of total sales
   - measuring 'lost revenue' from price discounting

5. types of customers receiving price reductions by numbers and amount
6. market shares in individual markets
7. present, forecast and target product costs with the following analysis:
   - design, purchasing, production, storage, marketing costs, etc
   - fixed, variable, semi-variable costs
8. product, unit and total contributions in different markets
9. price complaints from customers, and from salesmen
10. stocks of finished goods at different points in the distribution chain
11. customers' attitudes to the company's prices, packaging, etc
12. number of lost customers
13. numbers of enquiries and subsequent purchases—advertising/pricing 'hit' rate.

This type of system is forward looking and is likely to identify some of the shifts in demand that are occurring in the market place as well as identifying future trends in costs and product profitability.

The computer decision

The earlier discussion, under the heading of 'Systems Survey', indicated that the growth of the business or improvements in information technology, coupled with the need to maintain efficiency, may lead management to consider computerisation (or upgrading the present system); this section will review the advantages and disadvantages of computerisation before giving some guidance on the implementation of such a system.

Computerisation versus alternatives

The consideration of computerisation should be made only after a thorough analysis of the present methods employed. Questions, such as, 'Does the business need to computerise?', 'Are the present systems adequate?' or 'Will they handle business growth and for how long?' must be addressed in order to determine the need to computerise. It may be less costly to extend a manual system rather than to purchase a fully computerised system. An assessment of the means by which the company's current operation actually functions is needed so as to determine whether minor amendment or the implementation of several procedures is needed in order to achieve the desired results. The problem may be that the hardware and software currently used are not functioning correctly, or proper maintenance is not being performed. A close review of such factors could result in substantial cost savings as improved utilisation of current resources may provide the information that is required without the financial and personnel resources needed to implement new systems.

Although this section deals with the advantages and disadvantages of in-house computer systems, management should also be aware of other available processing alternatives such as computer bureaux which remove many of the problems of in-house processing. Moreover, a bureau may be used as a preliminary experiment for a computerised system prior to extensive expenditure on in-house computer equipment.

To consider whether an automated accounting system will be an asset to the growing business, the reasons for computerisation must be examined. Some of the advantages of computerisation include:

- improved clerical performance
- faster order processing
- faster billing
- improved processing of creditors
- improved stock control
- improved production planning
- improved control of sales effort.

In summary, a computer often permits the growing business improved control over its operations. In the production area, in customer services, in the sales department, in payroll; all may be linked through an integrated system. The company obtains information that, in all likelihood, was not provided before. Moreover, such information will now be provided in a more timely manner.

However, computerisation should never be seen as the panacea for all operational problems. A computer system requires discipline; if this is not applied to the computerisation process the end product will be both costly and not to original specification. Accordingly, consideration of when not to computerise is as equally important as to the computerisation process itself.

If any of the following situations exist at the time of the systems review, the installation of a computer system will be an arduous and time consuming process. The company should not computerise:

- if there are no systems to computerise
- if the operation lacks basic controls or if the nature of the business or industry is such that greater flexibility is required
- if there is a lack of commitment on the part of the managers—computerisation takes time, with the conversion being a slow, tedious and often frustrating process
- if there are staffing problems together with a reluctance to hire additional or competent people
- if the decision is based solely on cost reductions or if a fixed budget is set without knowledge of, or regard for, real costs.

Computerisation may be a viable alternative if the above problems are resolved in advance. With a reasonable understanding of current deficiencies management may proceed to the next step of integrating a computer into the information system. Since the core of most data processing systems is the ability to convert large quantities of data into useful information, management must firstly establish the information which is needed to run the operation more efficiently. A computer is no more than a means to an end and should be evaluated as such. There are advantages and disadvantages, benefits and costs to the installation of a computer. Only a detailed analysis of present and future operations will permit an informed business decision to be taken.

Reasons for using a computer

- frequently the more common reasons for management of a growing business wishing to computerise are subjective
  —management feel that they must 'keep up with competitors'
  —fear of pressure from competitors who use them
  —a belief that machines will resolve personnel problems

- improved clerical performance
  Although computerisation can reduce clerical work, the computer still requires input, and so clerical work is often merely reallocated. Computer salesmen often state that the clerical wage bill can be reduced; whilst this may occur eventually, such costs often *increase* during the conversion phase

- faster processing
  —faster processing and improved controls
  —faster shipments (eg computer-generated packing lists, packing orders, etc)
  —faster billing
    ... improved cash flow
  —reduced processing time for payables
    ... opportunity to take discounts
  —improved stock control
    ... faster posting (often as a by-product of invoicing)
    ... reduced stock levels through better turnover information as well as monitoring of slow moving items
  —improved production planning
    ... better scheduling
    ... reduced backlog
    ... reduced expediting
    ... cost control
  —improved control of sales effort through increased sales analyses and reporting
  —increased customer service through the ability to review customer records on-line and determine order status, invoices due, etc
  —improved insight into the business
    ... more information is available, contributing to improved analysis of profitability/efficiency
    ... it is integrated and can be analysed later in many different formats (eg manufacturer's job cost system)
    ... greater flexibility as to reports provided/available (especially if a report generator is available).

Although a growing company entering the computer arena for the first time may not have the organisational sophistication of a large established corporation, it may nevertheless be advised to adopt some large company techniques in planning for the installation of a computerised system. This process is described in more detail in the next section.

Implementation of computerised management information systems

The importance of harnessing information, in order to gain a competitive advantage in the market place, has been recognised for some time. However, evidence indicates that senior managers feel uncertain as to exactly how their systems and information provide them with a competitive edge. Traditionally, in the 1970s and early 1980s the introduction of computerised systems was justified on the basis of cost reduction, eg reduction in staffing numbers, working capital costs and so on. During the late 1980s, companies recognised that computerisation projects, which enhance the marketing capability, play a major part in providing a competitive edge in areas such as:

- sensitivity analysis tools in managing the marketing mix
- customer service and quality analysis
- image creation and
- computer assisted design.

Computer assisted design for use in product development and analysis of customer held data for sales targetting are two examples where Information Technology has assisted in creating an area of competitive advantage.

Traditionally, the growing organisation first encounters computing systems in the areas of:

- accounting packages
- statutory returns, eg Inland Revenue/Customs & Excise
- payroll modules
- sales analyses and credit control
- stock control/stock management
- fixed asset registers.

Primarily, computing is introduced to assist in compliance with statutory requirements or for internal management control, rather than for specific business growth. However, some of these systems may hold a wealth of information which, if utilised by management, could assist considerably in the growth of the business. Sales data is an example where information on customer profile, preference and so on is often maintained but is not exploited.

Business strategy considerations

Flexibility is required to survive in a dynamic competitive business environment. It is therefore essential for the growing business to ensure that information systems are themselves flexible and easy to understand and use. The impact of incorporating a number of acquisitions or speedy volume growth on a structured, cumbersome system may be detrimental to management's ability to plan and control its strategy.

A key element in implementing flexibility is the ability to underpin the business plan with information systems that assist in delivering the aims and objectives of that plan. The key to success in this area is recognising the relative priority of different types of information requirements and committing resources to implement the higher priority requirements. The overall message is that the management information system should be business, and not technology, driven.

Most organisations will operate at three different levels namely:

1. strategic (say 3–5 years)
2. tactical (say 1–12 months)
3. day-to-day.

It is the analysis of an organisation's information requirements, at each of these three levels, and the priority of information needs at each level which are fundamental to successfully identifying an information strategy. However, prior to formulating any long-term information strategy it is necessary to consider other business related issues, such as:

- organisational structure
- geographical location of decision making units and the impact upon telecommunications/networking
- existing computing skills and experience of end users and data processing personnel
- ability of management to direct investment in Information Technology and successfully manage the change.

Information technology (IT)

IT, in its widest context, has been falling in cost and has improved in functionality at a remarkable rate and this is likely to continue into the foreseeable future. However, even existing IT has not yet been exploited by management in a significant way.

The power and application of personal computers, distributed processing, telecommunications, etc have only been available on a large scale during the 1980s. Software tools which assist in decision making and support have also become more readily available during this period. How best to harness technology in the form of hardware, software and telecommunications in order to achieve the organisation's overall business objectives is critical in developing a competitive edge in the market place.

Implementation

Against this conceptual background of how a growing organisation should develop its information requirements, the dynamism of a growing organisation often requires a short-term solution to information requirements to address today's needs rather than tomorrow's objectives. However, once the IT long-term plan has been accepted, its implementation, in a controlled, timely and cost effective manner, is essential to the continued growth of the organisation. The high efficiency and cost benefit improvements in computer hardware in recent years have not always been mirrored by similar improvements in software productivity, particularly where complex information requirements and systems integration exist. Despite the introduction of fourth generation language and software engineering techniques, development of bespoke computer systems remains time consuming and costly. Package solutions which produce a close fit to the user's information requirements are often seen as the most cost effective way forward.

For expanding organisations, three factors influence system development:

- *business justification*   Cost benefit analyses for investment in computer systems are notoriously difficult. Not only are cost estimates frequently proved to be inaccurate, but benefits have often been regarded as intangible. In recent years this has changed. A more harsh economic climate has led to increased focus on investment returns, so that improved management information is now required to be reflected in increased revenues or reduced costs of working capital. Increased penetration of IT into operating areas, such as Electronic Point of Sale (EPOS) and office automation, has accentuated this trend
- *increased use of packaged software*   Conventional wisdom, that user requirements are paramount, has been modified in recent years with the increasing realisation that comparatively few requirements are totally inflexible. A better overall business solution is frequently possible if IT resources are regarded as a partnership with users, rather than as a service function
- *more sophisticated packages*   Software package suppliers generate profits through sales volume. In an effort to fit as broad a range of requirements as possible, suppliers have sought to allow customisation by increasing numbers of parameters and the use of flexible menus and report generators. As a result, many packages have come to resemble high-level languages, requiring increased systems development knowledge for implementation.

In seeking a package solution, many companies have clear plans for business development and are aware of the broad business areas where effective use of IT can assist them. Frequently, however, there is a shortage of in-house expertise to address the following areas:

- *project feasibility study*   Define business requirements in terms which allow packaged software to be evaluated
- *package selection*   Perform evaluation of packages to support investment proposals
- *implementation*   Implement the selected packages, including any necessary modifications
- *overall project management*   Commit sufficient management resources to the project to establish appropriate planning, monitoring and control mechanisms and to operate these mechanisms effectively.

In order to assist in the above processes the objectives and major tasks have been identified within each of the four areas referred to above. These can be used as a framework within which new packaged software may be evaluated and implemented.

Project feasibility study

OBJECTIVES

The project feasibility study phase is designed to:

- identify the projects where implementation of packaged software generates the highest return on investment
- quantify the investment returns
- identify the key business objectives which the project must satisfy.

MAJOR TASKS

The major tasks of this phase are to:

1. *organise and plan the assignment*   Responsibilities and reporting lines are defined and project control procedures established
2. *review business objectives*   Business plans are reviewed and key performance indicators identified for management control of the business areas under review. Critical success factors are defined to serve as a framework for systems development
3. *identify information needs*   The key information and processing needs required to manage the business areas are identified
4. *review current systems*   Current systems are critically assessed to develop further business knowledge and permit evaluation of staff resourcing and skills constraints
5. *define information systems*   Descriptions of information systems are prepared. The benefits of developing new systems are reviewed with management to allow initial prioritisation of projects
6. *evaluation technology options*   An initial review of potential technical solutions is prepared and a broad estimate of costs established on the basis of existing knowledge. This is used as the basis for the initial cost benefit analysis
7. *report to management*   Work to date and the resulting conclusions are summarised and recommendations for investment put forward in a report to management.

The major benefits from adopting such an approach ensure that:

- business objectives drive system development investments
- projects are prioritised and sequenced to maximise returns
- adequate investment appraisal is performed before significant expenditure is incurred
- projects are clearly defined in business terms to provide a framework for evaluation, selection and implementation.

Package selection phase

OBJECTIVE

The objective of this phase is to select an application package which meets business requirements because it:

- provides all the key benefits identified in the project feasibility study
- represents the best value for money.

The major tasks in the package selection phase are:

1. *project planning and organisation*   A working framework is established for the staff involved and activities required. This provides a basis for managing the selection process
2. *development of requirements definition*   This task involves extensive fact finding and structuring of the relevant information. Key systems requirements and benefits are identified at this stage, based on the business requirements of the system
3. *establishing evaluation criteria*   Requirements are weighted for importance and reviewed with management
4. *preparation of request for proposal*   The request for proposal is finalised as a basis for suppliers to submit proposed solutions, costs and timescales
5. *briefing of suppliers*   If necessary, a briefing conference is held for all suppliers who are asked to submit proposals
6. *evaluation of proposals*   Proposals are screened in order to shortlist selected solutions for in-depth evaluation
7. *in-depth evaluation*   Shortlisted proposals are evaluated in-depth, including surveys of existing customers and on-site visits to suppliers' sites
8. *vendor selection*   The preferred solution is finalised
9. *contract negotiation*   Detailed contract points are finalised
10. *report to management*   A report is prepared to management summarising the selection process and setting out the action now required
11. *contract completion*   Contracts are signed in preparation for implementation.

The major benefits from adopting such an approach are:

- the project team distinguishes critical from merely desirable features when evaluating possible packages
- comprehensive questionnaires assist in all stages of the selection process.

Implementation phase

The implementation phase is designed to assist in achieving timely and cost effective implementation of acquired systems to meet business needs.

The major tasks in the implementation phase are to:

1. *plan and organise the assignment*   Plans for the implementation phase are prepared as a basis for controlling the project and allocating

resources, which ensure project deadlines are met and system(s) delivered within budget

2. *define user requirements*   The user requirements prepared for the package selection phase are reviewed in the light of the package decision and the use of parameters, account codes and other user defined variables is decided

3. *prepare a detailed implementation plan*   Implementation plans are prepared to cover all aspects of installing the system

4. *finalise detailed requirement specifications*   Necessary modifications and interfaces to the basic package together with file conversion and initial data loading programs are specified. Forms and pre-printed stationery are designed and supplies are acquired. All package parameters and reporting formats are completed ready for testing

5. *install hardware*   All space planning, office services, installation and commissioning of equipment and fixtures and fittings is effected in both computer and user areas

6. *install software*   Package software and any custom developed software is installed ready for acceptance testing

7. *complete documentation and training*   All documentation necessary to supplement that supplied with the package is prepared. All personnel involved with the system are trained

8. *perform acceptance testing*   The system, including modifications, interfaces and conversion programs, is tested and approved

9. *implement the system*   All preparatory work for setting up the new systems files is performed. Controls over data on the new and old systems are reconciled and operational running established, after a period of parallel running if required

10. *perform a post-implementation review*   The live operation of the system is compared with original requirements and budget and deadline performance on the project analysed.

The major benefits from such an approach include:

- improved management control of implementation through the use of a structured approach. As a result, systems are more likely to be delivered on time and to budget and meet the original specification
- future support of the system by the provision of concise, cost-effective documentation should also reduce future maintenance costs and limit the risk of future systems downtime resulting from incomplete systems knowledge.

Overall project management

OBJECTIVES

Project management is designed to assist in meeting budgets and deadlines on projects. The services provided are the planning, monitoring and controlling of projects, including the reporting to senior management of progress against plan and budget.

MAJOR TASKS

The major tasks of project management are:

1. *setting project objectives*   In this task, the project objectives are formally established and the scope of the project defined
2. *determine project end products*   Major project anticipated benefits are identified and measures of success established
3. *setting project strategy*   This task determines the relationships, if any, with other projects, sets time and cost constraints and identifies project phases and related end products. In addition, project risks are assessed and contingency requirements set
4. *preparing the overall project plan*   In this task, project phases are analysed into activities and the effort for each activity estimated. Dependencies between activities are established and activities scheduled. An activity bar chart is produced for the overall project
5. *preparing task plans*   Activities are analysed into tasks and effort estimates; dependencies and scheduling are established at task level. A task bar chart is produced
6. *preparing project budgets*   Resources and cost budgets are produced
7. *creating a project organisation*   Roles and responsibilities can now be allocated, resources obtained and structured into teams
8. *directing the project team*   Responsibilities are delegated and teams supervised. Communication, co-ordination, motivation and counselling are the primary activities
9. *monitoring and reporting project progress*   Time, costs and quality are assessed and status reported.

The major benefits from using such an approach include:

- projects are more likely to be delivered on time and within budget
- problems will be identified earlier through better planning
- quality will be improved by review of task deliverables.

Conclusion

No matter how successful a business has been in terms of growth and development, it is virtually certain that if the management information systems have failed to develop in line with other sectors of the business, then the foundations upon which growth has been built will be undermined. In the dynamic environment in which the growing company operates, management's ability to develop and ultimately achieve its strategy will depend upon the existence of information upon which to base its decisions.

In this chapter we have stressed the need for information to be relevant for each level of decision-taker. In addition, the information should be reliable and timely, with care taken in system design not to overwhelm the user with superfluous or irrelevant information.

The chapter concentrates primarily on the basics of systems analysis, and consideration of the ongoing development of accounting systems with specific consideration of costing and pricing systems. Clearly, a company's overall management information system must also produce information of a quasi-financial nature if all disciplines within the company are to be able to work toward the corporate strategy. Accordingly, succeeding chapters consider various information aspects appertaining to the marketing, production and human resource functions.

CHAPTER 3

Financing Growth

Introduction

One of the principal constraints frequently faced by the growing company is
a lack of finance. This arises not only with respect to the capital expenditure
aspects of growth but also, just as importantly, to the working capital
requirements of the rapidly growing business.

For growth to be both achieved and sustained, management will need to
develop a sound working knowledge of the basic principles of funding. Only
then can financial planning be undertaken in a considered and co-ordinated
fashion so as to safeguard and build upon the strategy for growth.

The alternative sources of finance and wide-ranging types of financial
instruments currently available can, initially, seem overwhelming to financially inexperienced management. Seeking the most appropriate form of
finance may entail considerable research and negotiation prior to successful
conclusion. However, an understanding of the most commonly used sources
of finance is an essential first step for the entrepreneur wishing to raise
additional finance or utilise existing resources as beneficially as possible.

The chapter is organised under six headings:

1. principles of funding
2. wholly secured funding
3. venture capital
4. public listing
5. other sources of funding
6. working capital management.

Principles of funding

Any potential provider of finance would wish to ensure that the return
obtained on an investment corresponds with the risks associated with
making that investment—for example, equity investment will command a
higher rate of return than secured debt. The growing business should
endeavour to obtain the most appropriate type of finance for any particular
situation and an important aspect of this is that the cost of funds to the
business (whether it be interest, dividends or equity foregone) should be
matched as closely as possible to the overall requirement. An overdraft, for
instance, can be an efficient means of financing fluctuating working capital
requirements as the interest cost is calculated on a daily basis.

Funding requirements will not only vary from company to company, but
also, within any given business there may be a variety of different funding

needs. These may initially be categorised according to the duration for which the funds will be required, ie over the short, medium, or long-term. Management should determine the timing of any funding requirement from the company's cashflow forecast and, after a consideration of the available security and repayment requirements, it should be possible to identify the most appropriate types and sources of finance.

Typically, the cashflow forecasts will show a fluctuating profile (see Fig 3.1 on page 52). Once the peak borrowing requirement has been identified the next step should be to determine whether there is a lower limit below which borrowings will not fall. The difference between this lower limit and the peak requirement represents an approximation of the short-term funding requirement. The remainder of the funding requirement may be termed 'hard-core' and medium or long-term finance should be considered.

The process of identifying an appropriate funding source is illustrated by Fig 3.2 on page 53. Clearly this represents something of an over-simplification and there will be a number of overlaps between short/medium and medium/long-term requirements. However, this approach does provide a framework around which to construct an overview of the various sources of finance available to the growing company.

Wholly secured funding

Bank loans and overdrafts are the most common source of secured finance, and the cost of such finance will reflect the lender's perception of the risks involved, as well as prevailing market rates of interest. An immature company can frequently expect to pay a higher rate of interest than a business with a proven track record, but a lender may reduce the risk (and hence the cost) associated with a debt by increasing the tangible security that he takes over the company's assets.

This security may be obtained by means of either fixed or floating charge (or a combination of both) over the assets and undertaking of the business. A fixed charge relates to a specifically identified asset of the business (such as property) whereas a floating charge relates to a class of business assets, such as stock, where the separable items within the class will change over time. In the case of medium and long-term finance the security will ideally be of a permanent and non-wasting form such as a freehold or long leasehold premises and here a legal mortgage may be sought.

In a situation where security is taken over the company's operating assets such as debtors or stock, the lender will normally seek reliable monthly or quarterly management accounts from the business. This facilitates an on-going re-assessment of the adequacy of the security against the level of borrowings, as well as ensuring that the providers of finance are kept up to date with the trading performance of the business.

When making an assessment of the available security, a bank manager will base a mortgage debenture valuation upon the balance sheet of the company. In carrying out this exercise much depends on the banker's judgement of the business, its management, its assets and potential. Moreover, a bank will not usually lend against security in isolation, but will endeavour to ensure that the cashflow projections appear achievable and demonstrate an ability to discharge repayments of capital and interest as they fall due.

Fig 3.1: Example of a Possible Cashflow Forecast

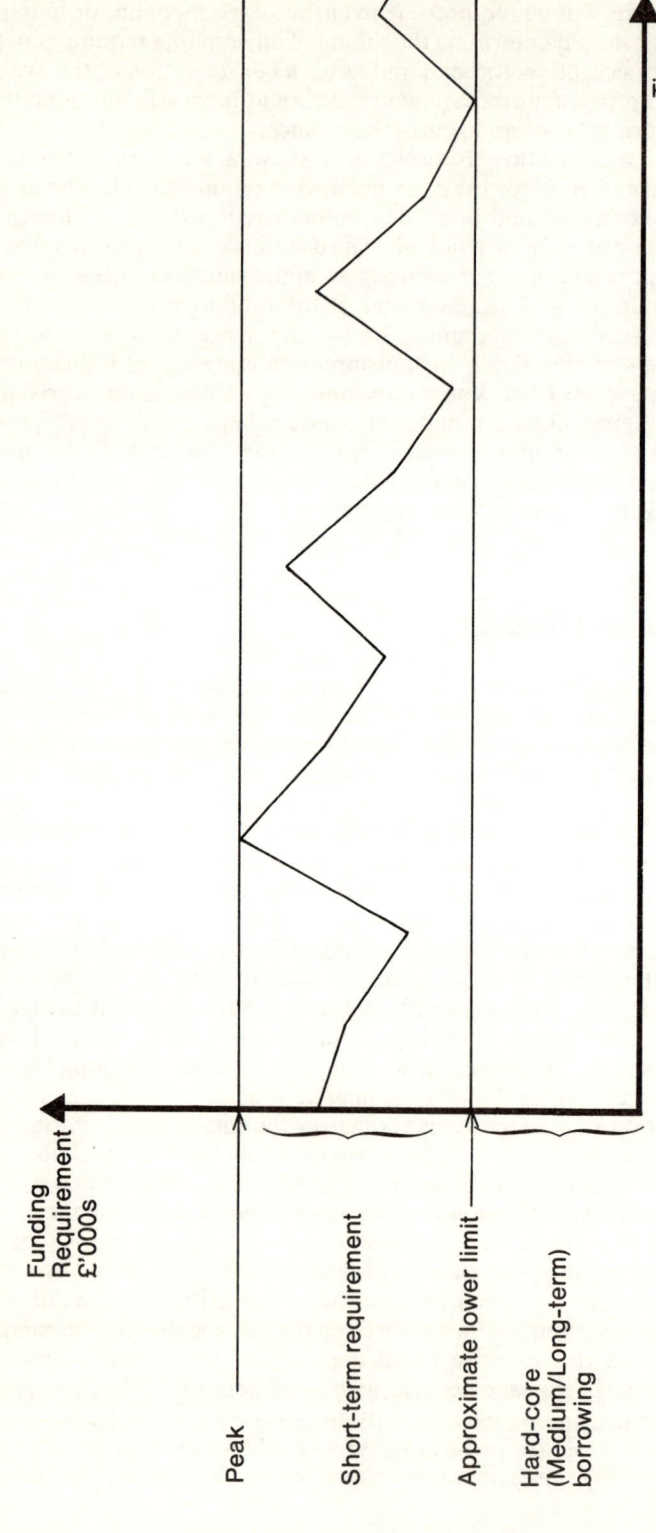

Funding
Requirement
£'000s

Time

Peak

Short-term requirement

Approximate lower limit

Hard-core
(Medium/Long-term)
borrowing

Fig 3.2: Principles of Funding

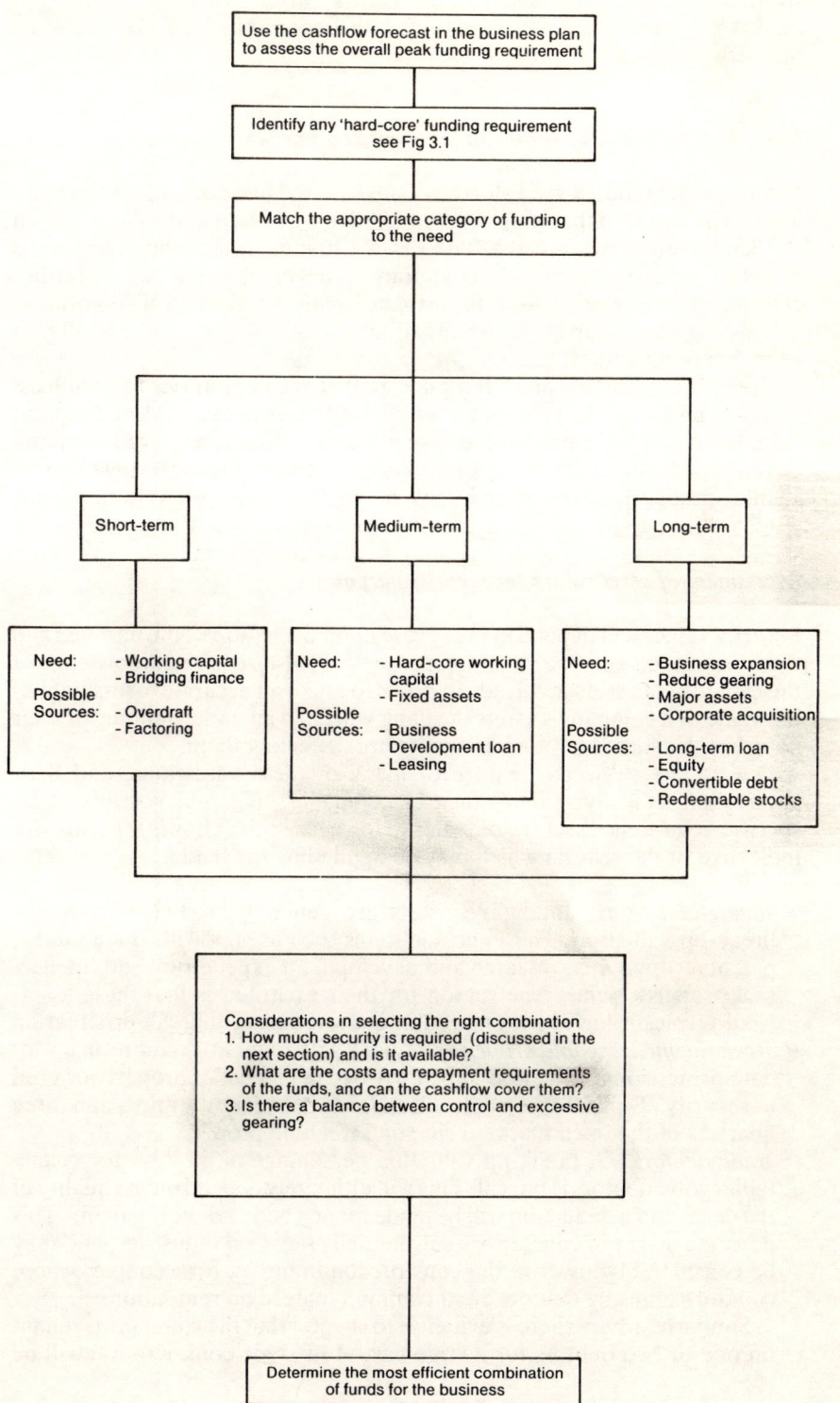

Use the cashflow forecast in the business plan to assess the overall peak funding requirement

Identify any 'hard-core' funding requirement see Fig 3.1

Match the appropriate category of funding to the need

Short-term

Need: - Working capital
       - Bridging finance
Possible
Sources: - Overdraft
         - Factoring

Medium-term

Need: - Hard-core working
         capital
       - Fixed assets
Possible
Sources: - Business
           Development loan
         - Leasing

Long-term

Need: - Business expansion
       - Reduce gearing
       - Major assets
       - Corporate acquisition
Possible
Sources: - Long-term loan
         - Equity
         - Convertible debt
         - Redeemable stocks

Considerations in selecting the right combination
1. How much security is required (discussed in the next section) and is it available?
2. What are the costs and repayment requirements of the funds, and can the cashflow cover them?
3. Is there a balance between control and excessive gearing?

Determine the most efficient combination of funds for the business

The paragraphs which follow are intended solely as a general guide to the approach which a bank manager *might* take when estimating the available security in a company's balance sheet. The approach will tend to vary from bank to bank and clearly variations will occur with respect to specific industry practices.

Basis and frequency of valuation for security purposes

Mortgage debentures are valued by banks on the basis of a break-up valuation. The assets of the company are effectively assessed at the values which the lender estimates are realisable in a situation where the company is unable to meet its repayment obligations. Gross break-up values are further reduced by estimated realisation costs and by any preferential claims prior to calculating a break-up valuation. Realisation costs might typically be 10% of gross break-up values.

Break-up valuations are often calculated at regular intervals and at least annually by the bank on receipt of an audited balance sheet. More frequent valuations may be made where management accounts are available, and generally whenever evidence of a change in asset values is judged to be significant, eg where there are known major asset acquisitions or disposals.

Assessment of asset values for security purposes

Security values will depend in every case upon the nature of the business and the assets involved. The valuation process will also require a knowledge of the category of assets involved. In order to make an accurate assessment of the value of a company's assets the bank will need an understanding of their nature, substance, and the business factors affecting them.

Due to the subjective nature of many of these valuations, and their application to a diversified range of companies, it is not possible to be specific regarding asset value rules. However, the following points are indicative of the criteria which may be applied by the lender:

- *intangible assets*   Intangible assets are generally excluded from any break-up valuation. These include items such as goodwill, trade marks, patents, copyrights, research and development expenditure and intellectual property rights. The reason for their exclusion is that these assets would typically have little or no value in a forced sale or break-up situation
- *freehold and leasehold property*   A bank will frequently require an up-to-date professional valuation to be provided in respect of property offered as security. Typically the bank will advance between two thirds and three quarters of the open market value of a freehold property
- *trade debtors*   A break-up valuation percentage of 60–70% for collectable, good debtors is typical. This will ultimately depend on the quality of the debts and a deduction will be made for any bad or doubtful items. This percentage can of course vary substantially between industries, and may be considerably lower in the construction industry, for example, where counter-claims by debtors are a common feature on realisation.

  Similarly, where there is evidence to suggest that the company is reliant on one or two debtors for a large part of its trade consideration will be given to reducing the percentage in recognition of the potentially increased risk. Enquiries as to the debtor's financial standing may be sought

- *stock* A break-up valuation is difficult to estimate since it will depend on such factors as market demand for the relevant goods and the resale value of stock components. Where stock is old or of poor quality, a heavy discount will be applied. Typically, however, a break up valuation of 30% would be used in most cases although this may be reduced to 10% for certain industries such as construction.

  Consideration is also given to the possible impact of reservation of title clauses on stock values. Essentially, if a supplier has such a clause in his conditions of sale, then in the event of a liquidation or administrative receivership he may be entitled to claim for the return of goods or even return of the proceeds of sale of the goods. Although such claims are often difficult to substantiate, if successful, they would rank in priority to a bank's floating charge and thus impair the bank's security. It is likely that the lender will apply a deduction for stocks supplied under such contracts when calculating gross break-up values

- *work in progress* Where work in progress is separately identified, it will normally be entered in the debenture valuation at nil, recognising that in the event of liquidation it is unlikely that such an asset would be realisable. Heavy manufacturing industry is an example where this would often apply

- *plant and machinery* A break-up valuation percentage of approximately 20% of book value may be typical although this will vary substantially depending on the assets involved.

  Amounts outstanding under hire purchase or leasing agreements will be deducted from the gross break-up value of plant and machinery, since the lessor will have a charge over the specific assets covered by these financing agreements.

  Where plant and machinery accounts for a high proportion of total assets, consideration may be given to obtaining a professional valuation. For example, this may be worthwhile for businesses in the plant and tool hire sector. This may also be appropriate when plant and machinery is of a specialist nature, often resulting in a book value which does not accurately reflect market value.

The entrepreneur frequently comes into conflict with the conventional banker over the conservative valuation applied to the company's assets for security purposes. It should be remembered, however, that the lender is prudently assuming a worst case scenario when advancing funds based purely on security backing. He views it from the perspective of whether funds would be recoverable in the event of the company no longer operating as a going concern—hence the discounts applied. Conversely, however, the entrepreneur traditionally applies somewhat less than conservative valuations to the assets involved as he assumes that a cessation of trade is unlikely.

Personal guarantees

In certain instances, depending upon the value of the assets held by the business, the directors may also be asked to provide personal guarantees to secure funding for the company. This may involve providing a mortgage over personal assets, such as private homes, as security for the guarantee. In such cases it is essential that the directors fully comprehend the liability they are taking on and their responsibilities thereunder.

Overdrafts versus loans

Having viewed the criteria which a bank might apply when assessing the available security and, assuming that the bank manager is satisfied by the cashflow forecasts, management may then be faced by a choice of loan, overdraft or a combination of the two supported by debenture and/or guarantees.

Overdrafts are frequently simple to arrange and are widely used to fund short-term fluctuating working capital needs. As interest only accrues on the debt outstanding at any point in time this can be the least costly form of debt finance available, with rates usually varying between 1.5% and 4% over base rate, depending on the status of the company. The rate is unlikely to vary substantially between banks, and rates below 1.5% over base can usually only be negotiated by major corporates. A disadvantage of over-drafts is that they are regularly reviewed by the bank, which can result in uncertainty for the business as regards availability of finance for the medium or long-term. (In theory they are also repayable on demand but this is a sanction seldom exercised by the lender under normal trading conditions.)

Whilst not necessarily suffering from this uncertainty, term loans can, however, be inflexible especially if not carefully negotiated, and there may be additional drawbacks:

1. the company may suffer interest on a sum which is not always fully required, due to periodic cash surpluses
2. there is a potential risk of suffering from a high fixed interest rate when market rates are actually falling
3. it may be difficult and expensive to alter the funding package once it is in place.

Careful choice of the appropriate loan option can, however, mitigate these drawbacks, and in recent years banks have substantially expanded the range of loans they can offer. Features now include a wide choice of loan periods, capital repayment holidays, deferred interest terms and even a 'bullet' repayment which comprises a single full repayment at the end of the loan term.

It is always worthwhile discussing and negotiating each aspect of the financing package to ensure it fully reflects the requirements and cashflow of the business, rather than simply accepting a standard loan product.

Before giving consideration to unsecured finance, in the form of venture or development capital, a brief outline of two other common sources of secured funds is given below.

Leasing

A lease is a contract under which one party, the lessor, owns an asset which is made available for use by another party, the lessee, in consideration for periodic rental payments. Leases fall into two distinct categories:

1. finance leases
2. operating leases.

Under a finance lease agreement the lessee acquires substantially all the benefits of the use of an asset for the greater part of its useful economic life, and takes on substantially all of the risks associated with ownership. In economic substance it is similar to the purchase of an asset even though legal title to the asset remains with the lessor. At the end of the lease period there may be a provision in the agreement for extension at peppercorn rent or the right to buy the asset outright for a negligible consideration. An operating lease may be for short or long periods, but a possibility is that the lessor will lease the asset to other parties during its economic life. Often such leases contain short notice termination provisions which are not found in finance leases.

Funds presently 'frozen', through a company's self-financing of fixed assets, may be released under a 'sale and leaseback' arrangement where the asset is sold to a lessor and then leased back by the vendor. Thereby resulting in a one-off cash benefit, followed by a stream of lease rentals.

In practice, leasing may be a flexible source of finance and often plays a major role in corporate funding. It enables management to alleviate the cashflow impact of capital expenditure which might otherwise involve, for example, increasing the equity base of the business.

Factoring

Under this method of finance a factoring house will, typically, handle the administration of a company's sales ledger and provide cash against a percentage of the sales invoice value. Factoring is often used for financing in rapid sales growth situations, since it reduces the working capital requirements which arise from timing differences between incurring cost of sales and actually receiving cash from debtors. Key features of factoring include:

1. sales ledger administration is combined with a funding facility, frequently up to 80% of the value of a sales invoice
2. the factor collects trade debts and remits to the business all sums not previously given by way of advance net of his own charges
3. the larger factors, many of whom are owned by major banks, offer non-recourse facilities where the factor incurs the cost of bad debts. This can be of benefit to small and medium sized companies although the factor's opinion as to the creditworthiness of the company's customers may restrict the amount he is prepared to advance in this situation
4. the interest charged on amounts advanced by the factor are similar to bank overdraft rates, while the sales ledger administration, inclusive of bad debt protection, will generally cost between 0.75% and 2.5% of turnover, depending on the volume of work involved.

A further debt finance option is 'invoice discounting'. This again is primarily used as a means of raising funds against specific debts although the company retains control of the sales ledger and credit control procedures.

It should always be remembered, when considering the use of a factor, that the security available to cover any bank overdraft will be reduced if the trade debtors are released to cover the factoring facilities.

Venture capital

There are many examples where companies have funded growth solely by the use of factoring, term loans or other secured sources of finance. As long as the cost and risks associated with gearing are not unduly onerous this approach may be totally acceptable.

There will, however, be many examples where debt finance is not available or is inappropriate for the specific funding requirement due to, for example, the level of risk inherent in the business or resulting from a lack of security, or fluctuating cashflow. In this instance, so as to obtain sufficient funding, management may have to offer a percentage of the company equity to a financier in return for the latter's acceptance of the risks involved.

Third party 'risk capital', such as this, is also known as 'Venture Capital'. The provision of such finance has grown substantially in the UK over the past decade, to the point where there are now approximately 130 organisations with available investment funds estimated at £4.5 billion. These funds have proven to be a significant source of funding for the growing business.

Definition and characteristics

A broad definition of venture capital might be 'the provision of longer-term risk finance by a third party with the primary intention of making above average returns'. There are four characteristics which distinguish venture capital:

1. there is usually a degree of equity participation
2. the funds are normally unsecured
3. often the major element of the venture capitalist's return arises by way of capital gain and eventual realisation of his equity stake (the 'exit' point). Part of the return may come from a 'running yield' (dividends and interest) on the investment
4. the venture capitalist normally adopts a more 'hands-on' approach to the investment than a provider of conventional debt, such as a bank. This involvement, whilst obviously providing the venture capitalist with some confidence, is not intended to restrict management but rather to complement it through active participation.

These characteristics are necessarily of a general nature as within the venture capital industry there is a wide range of individual firms offering different funding packages to various sectors of commerce on a whole range of terms. Many have market sector preferences, investment size and return criteria and each has an individual style of handling its portfolio.

Venture capital versus development capital

A distinction between venture and development capital can be made.

'Venture' capital describes start-up or early stage financing, including seed capital. Seed capital investment frequently finances research and development into new technology prior to a product launch. This is the smallest sector of the venture capital market, in terms of value of deals, and this type of finance is provided by only a limited number of venture capital funds. The sector is characterised by high risk. Past experience of investors suggests a significant failure rate, which will clearly affect the return sought by the venture capitalist on such deals.

'Start up and other early stage financing' is used to describe funds employed in initiating production or the provision of a service and commencement of trading. It may also be difficult to raise finance within this category as a lack of track record may distort an investor's evaluation of risk. The reluctance of investors in this area has led to the perception of a 'funding gap' in the market place. The disproportionate level of monitoring required by the investor, allied to a high business failure rate, accounts for a discernible drift away from younger high growth companies into larger and, what are perceived as, lower risk investments. Whilst the venture capital industry would claim that there is finance available for a sufficiently attractive proposition, it is certainly reasonable to assume that a start-up company will experience more difficulty in securing funds than a more mature business.

'Development' capital is that funding which is applied to the expansion of established businesses with a proven track record and, possibly, with existing venture capital investment in place ('second-round financing'). The term is often used to embrace the finance which funds management buy-outs (MBOs) or buy-ins (MBIs).

Development capital is usually sought by companies as a means of financing a major stage in development. Typical examples would be:

1. refinancing a capital structure which is no longer appropriate
2. corporate acquisitions or development of new products/markets
3. expansion of activities which may involve improvements in facilities such as premises, plant or machinery. This can often be effected in conjunction with an element of debt finance
4. enabling the entrepreneur to realise a proportion of his investment in the company.

Because there is a track record for the company and/or the management team, the perceived risks associated with this type of investment are usually considered to be less.

Although there are conceptual differences between different classes of risk capital, in practice the general principles behind venture and development capital correspond closely, and hereafter 'venture capital' is used as an all encompassing phrase to also include development capital.

Advantages and disadvantages of venture capital finance

Prior to seeking venture capital finance, management should be aware of a number of advantages and disadvantages, a summary of which is given below:

ADVANTAGES

- *enlargement of capital base*   An enlarged capital base may enhance a company's standing with its bankers, customers and suppliers, thereby enabling more competitive prices or other market advantages to be obtained
- *reduced servicing costs*   Since the provider of venture capital is frequently more concerned with achieving a capital gain, the cost of servicing the funds may well be less than that arising on debt capital
- *finance is unsecured*   This may permit further debt to be raised as the company can increase borrowings and maintain an acceptable debt to equity ratio
- *availability of further finance*   Once a venture capital organisation has invested in a company it may prove to be a useful source to management in assessing new opportunities and, depending upon the outcome of the assessment, may contribute towards the financing of such projects
- *availability of non-executive directors*   Many venture capital investors require representation on the board of directors. This may provide an ideal opportunity for the original management team to strengthen the board's expertise in a specific area, to increase its circle of contacts and to obtain an independent and constructive view of their activities.

DISADVANTAGES

- *dilution of control*   The rewards in providing venture capital are usually achieved through the ownership of equity in the company. The entrepreneur will almost inevitably have to accept a reduced share of the business equity
- *greater accountability*   So as to monitor his investment the venture capital financier will require regular management information. This could, conversely, be viewed as a benefit as this imposes on management the discipline of producing prompt, reliable data
- *future expectations*   The majority of venture capital funds require an 'exit route' for their investments (ie they will wish to be assured that there is good potential for realisation of their stake in the company by sale or buy-back, for instance). This may take place at a date or using a mechanism which does not necessarily accord with management's long-term plans. For instance the fund may press for a public flotation at a time that is not necessarily ideal from the company's long-term point of view
- *fees*   There are associated costs arising from raising venture capital. These may, initially, be greater than those associated with debt since extra due diligence examination will be necessary.

It is essential that the management team seeking venture capital is aware of, and assesses, these implications prior to approaching any funds. The following key aspects should also be considered to assist in creating a beneficial and profitable relationship with an investing partner:

1. *reputation of the venture capital fund*   The entrepreneur will need to be assured that the potential financiers have a proven track record and an investment handling team that is experienced in the relevant business sector
2. *degree of involvement*   As previously noted, this will vary between venture capital funds. Some will require board representation and the individual in question, who may not necessarily be an employee of the fund, should be accepted by management, since he will become an integral part of the team and be expected to make a useful contribution to the business.

   Other funds may adopt a more passive approach, and, although reserving the right to appoint a director, may well be prepared to receive periodic financial information only
3. *flexibility*   It is important that the entrepreneur finalises a funding package that best suits the company's and his individual requirements. Since many deals usually entail the venture capitalist taking a significant equity stake, it is important to choose a structure that will neither unduly prejudice the cashflow of the business, at a time when it may be least able to pay, nor dominate the shareholding of the entrepreneur. It is also critical at this point for the entrepreneur to establish the capability of the venture capital fund to provide second-round finance if there is the possibility of an additional requirement a few years hence
4. *exit routes*   It is sensible, at the earliest stage, for both entrepreneur and venture capitalist to consider the latter's desired exit route. An ideal time horizon should be agreed in principle and an indication obtained of the means by which the investor sees his equity being realised. Typically, this will be via flotation of the company or by a trade sale. Buy-back provisions can often be built into an agreement if the entrepreneur so requires
5. *chemistry*   Both the entrepreneur and venture capitalist will be participating in a partnership. Positive and professional relationships should not be underestimated as a factor contributing to a successful partnership and it is important that both parties feel able to work together in a spirit of mutual trust and co-operation.

Approaching a venture capitalist

Venture capital is typically provided by insurance companies, pension funds, banks, and investment houses either directly (through their own funds) or indirectly (through specialist independent funds).

The funds have widely differing investment criteria and a problem that will face management is which of the available sources to choose.

An accountant or other advisor should be able to assist in locating a source of venture capital to suit the specific needs of the business. Clearly an institution with the relevant industry specialisation will be able to assess the risks and rewards of a business with greater skill and understanding.

Before contacting the venture capitalist, a brief oral presentation should be prepared. This should include a clear summary of the proposal and the reasons why management consider their business is a success both now, and more importantly in the future. A well-structured business plan (see

Chapter 1) is a prerequisite if the financiers are to make a reasonable assessment of the potential of the company.

It is important to note that raising venture capital is not an instantaneous process and will often take up to two to three months to complete. The investor will wish to perform 'due diligence' work, whereby as much information as possible will be gathered on the key individuals, the business and the industry in which it operates prior to an offer being made final. Moreover, there will often be a negotiation stage before the final terms of the package are agreed and there will be legal formalities, such as share issues, to complete. The key message is that a company should, as soon as possible, anticipate any future funding requirement so that the finance can be arranged in good time and on optimum terms.

The venture capital investor will assess a potential investment in four key areas:

1. management ability
2. market potential
3. competition
4. returns.

Management ability   Venture capitalists primarily support management, rather than the company itself or its products. If a company or product is successful, it is usually the result of management's expertise, competence and determination. If the venture capitalist has any security, it is his confidence in the ability of management to safeguard his, and their own, investment. Management's past experience is therefore a critical factor to the venture capitalist.

The investor will also wish to see a balanced management team in place that possesses the requisite technical, financial, organisational and marketing skills to guide the company towards continued growth. The business plan should specify how the individual talents of the management team will contribute to the company's success. If the management team lacks any basic skills the plan must demonstrate the means by which this is to be rectified, whether by recruitment, training, or temporary reliance on outside consultants.

Market potential   Where a company's products are to be sold in an existing market, that market should normally be growing and the products should, ideally, have some differentiating characteristics. Where the products are to be sold in a new market, considerable research will be required to demonstrate that sufficient market capacity exists to ensure the product's viability. Investors, understandably, are reluctant to back companies whose products or services rely on gaining market share from established and successful competitors. In addition to demonstrating that a market exists for the product, management must show that they have a strategy to penetrate that market.

Competition   A concise and accurate appraisal of current and potential competition will add credibility to the business plan. Prior to investment, a venture capitalist will make a thorough assessment of this and it will increase his confidence in the management team if the risks, that he independently perceives from competitive forces, accord with those already identified in the plan and are taken into account in the corporate strategy.

Returns   After investigating the above three areas the venture capitalist will have made an assessment of the key risk areas in the company. He will then attempt to match his potential returns to the level of risk involved, within the framework of a commercially attractive deal.

Venture capitalists often use an Internal Rate of Return (IRR) when assessing potential investments. This is the discount rate which, when applied to the forecast income stream from an investment, will result in a Net Present Value (NPV) of nil. The income stream will be in the form of a running yield, ie coupon on shares or interest on debt, and capital gain, eg any redemption premium on preferences shares (see below) or profit on the sale of ordinary shares. The financial projections in the company's business plan will be used as a starting point for the calculation of the IRR, but investors will normally make a risk adjustment to these figures depending on the outcome of their evaluations. It is not possible to be specific as to the level of return which will be sought, but a 'target' IRR of between 30% and 60% pa would be fairly typical. The venture capitalist will apply his target IRR to the risk adjusted forecast income stream, to determine the minimum stake in the company which he must take. A simple example of this evaluation of a company for the purposes of taking an equity stake is included in Appendix A on page 142.

The financial package

Once a venture capitalist has agreed to invest it is usually possible to draw together several sources of finance. In addition to the injection of venture capital, there may be included 'conventional' sources of funds such as secured loans and overdrafts, a capital expenditure facility from a lessor or a government grant or loan. Indeed, the most common approach is to determine (by reference to the cashflow forecasts and available security) the level of such conventional debt supportable by the business and then 'top up' the remaining requirement with venture capital, in this way the funds at risk are minimised. Often this 'risk money' will be offered by the venture capitalist in a mixture of various financial instruments. The three main types are ordinary shares, preference shares and unsecured loans.

Ordinary shares rank after preference shares and loans in their rights over the assets of the company in a liquidation. They tend nearly always to carry voting rights (and so ordinary shareholders are the owners of the business) but may have differing dividend entitlements depending on the company's Articles of Association. An example is that deferred ordinary shares, for instance, might not carry a dividend entitlement for a predetermined period.

Preference shares can have a variety of characteristics but do not normally carry the right to vote. They normally yield a fixed coupon rate but can, in the case of participating preference shares, be entitled to a further share of profits. Preference shares can also be cumulative, whereby dividend arrears will accumulate until there is sufficient cash and distributable profits in the company to pay them. Sometimes a conversion and/or redemption feature is included, which permits holders of preference shares eventually either to become ordinary shareholders or to realise their investment. The redemption of preference shares is essentially a repayment of those shares by the company. The preference shareholders may be entitled to a repayment amount in excess of the original cost of the shares—the redemption premium; in this way the venture capitalist is provided with a capital gain.

Some venture capitalists may include an unsecured loan within the package. Often referred to as 'mezzanine finance', this is an instrument which lies somewhere between equity and secured debt, since it can incorporate features of both and is designed to bridge the different risk positions of traditional equity and debt. The rates of return on mezzanine finance would currently be between 20% and 25% per annum reflecting the fact that the associated risks are higher than with secured finance but lower than with pure equity. Mezzanine might take the form of unsecured, subordinated debt with a high running yield or, alternatively, it may feature a relatively low coupon supplemented by means of an 'equity kicker' in the form of an option to convert the debt into ordinary shares.

Many financial packages incorporate the use of a 'ratchet'. This is a mechanism for providing the management team with an incentive to improve results by adjusting their percentage of the final equity in line with a pre-determined scale related to performance. The venture capitalist will often structure the ratchet such that his target IRR is preserved by providing him with an increased share in a less valuable business, in the event of a performance below budget (and vice versa for an improved performance).

Typically, under such a situation, the venture capitalist will issue preference shares that can be converted into ordinary shares at variable rates, based upon the company's achievement of pre-determined performance targets. If the targets are exceeded, then the conversion rate will be correspondingly lower for the investor, and the founders retain a larger percentage of the equity than otherwise. If properly applied, a ratchet is beneficial to all parties but targets must be set with care so that long-term objectives are not sacrificed simply to meet short-term performance targets.

It is common for all the investor's convertible funding instruments to be converted into equity or redeemed prior to an exit. However, the venture capitalist may not always wish to realise the whole of his investment. He may be keen to retain involvement in the continuing growth and potential of the business. Often this will also be attractive to the management team, since a close working relationship may have developed and the ongoing association may be valued.

Public listing

A further major means of financing expansion in the growing company is to seek a flotation on either the Unlisted Securities Market (USM) or obtain a full listing on the Official List of the Stock Exchange. Moreover, flotation is an ideal exit route for a venture capitalist as his stake in the business can be sold when the company's shares are offered to the public.

The USM was launched by the Stock Exchange in 1980 with the aim of providing a market with less stringent and less costly entry requirements than those of a full listing. It was primarily designed to meet the needs of smaller companies who had previously experienced difficulty in raising public finance. As well as reduced entry costs and less rigourous administration procedures, the USM is distinguished from the listed market by lower capitalisation values and a reduced percentage of equity capital (10% rather than 25%) that must be in public hands when dealings commence. To date, 770 companies have been admitted to the USM, of which over 130 have progressed to the main market.

A flotation on either market ensures a number of changes for a company and the principal of these are listed below:

1. *new sources of capital*   A flotation enables a company to raise equity from a larger pool of potential shareholders. Further capital may be obtained on an ongoing basis by such methods as rights issues
2. *funding acquisitions*   Acquisitions can be funded by using the company's own marketable shares as consideration
3. *realising an investment*   Once quoted, the marketability of a company's shares enables entrepreneurs (and venture capitalists) to dispose of shares if they desire, thereby obtaining a cash return from the growth of the business
4. *enhanced status*   Having satisfied entry requirements the public status of a company tends to be enhanced when dealing with banks, customers and suppliers. This improved profile can accelerate sales growth and enhance profitability by heightening public awareness of the company, its management and its products
5. *public scrutiny*   The market may expect steadily increasing profit trends and fluctuations can often result in sharp share price movements. This may tend to pressurise management into the achievement of short-term results at the expense of more beneficial long-term performance
6. *disclosure requirements*   Rigorous disclosure requirements must be followed as required by Stock Exchange regulations, such as shareholders' notification and approval of major acquisitions and disposals.

Suitability of a company for flotation

The primary responsibility for determining a company's suitability for flotation rests with the sponsor, usually a merchant bank or stockbroker. The company will often be introduced to a potential sponsor by way of a recommendation from one of its other professional advisors, and the sponsor will assess the company in detail to determine if it is a realistic flotation candidate.

The matters which will be considered include:

- the formal requirements of the Stock Exchange/USM
- the likely attractiveness to the market of the company's profit record and prospects
- the strength and integrity of its management
- the adequacy of its accounting systems and reporting procedures.

It may be that a final decision will depend on the contents of a detailed report on the business prepared by a firm of independent accountants, although a preliminary assessment by the company's sponsor is likely to be made at the outset to avoid unnecessary delay and cost to the company.

For an established company a pre-tax profit level of £500,000 is an approximate guide to the minimum profitability which would render the company's shares marketable on the USM, but this is not prescriptive and the past profit records of companies floated on the USM have varied greatly. There should always, however, be sufficient evidence to persuade prospective investors that there is a maintainable level of profits and an adequately financed business with growth prospects.

Other sources of funding

Additional methods of finance are available for growing companies in certain specialised situations. These are briefly summarised below under the following headings:

1. government and local authority grants
2. corporate venturing
3. finance for overseas trading.

Government and local authority grants

Most grant schemes are discretionary and the onus is generally upon the applicant to demonstrate the need for assistance and the benefit that is likely to accrue to the business and, if appropriate, the community. Grants arise on a variety of bases such as geographical location, type of project, training of personnel, etc and application is usually by way of a formal application through the government department administering the grant or loan. In Appendix B (page 144) a list has been provided of a number of the major grants currently available. If management believes that the company may be entitled to a grant they should contact either their professional advisors or the relevant government department direct.

Corporate venturing

Corporate venturing occurs where there is an investment of cash and management resources by one business in another. A corporate venturer has different criteria from those of the venture capitalist when reviewing a potential investment. The latter is concerned mainly with the return to be derived from the company whereas the former may perceive the following additional non-financial factors:

- access to developing technologies in related areas of activity
- a low cost diversification into new products and markets
- a continued awareness of competitive activity
- a future long-term partner or potential acquisition candidate.

The investee venture partner benefits through the following advantages:

- often the investor will be in the same industry sector and will be familiar with the market and the risks. The investee may not therefore have to 'educate' the investor when negotiating with him to invest

- management skills that may be lacking in the investee business can be obtained from the venture partner
- a corporate venturer will usually seek a minority shareholding which may be as low as 20% or less
- the investee business may be able to take advantage of the investor's existing marketing and distribution networks, thereby increasing its product's exposure in the market place
- the partnership may provide access to more competitive suppliers and pricing, and may even result in an introduction to the investor company's customer base.

It is important that the investee business considers the longer-term implications of the association. Assuming the venture is profitable the investor may well wish to acquire the balance of the investee's shares and this eventual option should be discussed by both parties at the outset.

Finance for overseas trading

Often, one of the most risky and complex areas of a company's operations is with respect to overseas trading. The problems of credit control and foreign currency exposure can, if not carefully addressed, act as substantial barriers to growth. The following paragraphs deal with the more common methods of minimising the risks associated with overseas trade.

- *foreign currency bank account* Where invoices are raised in foreign currency, it is often preferable to operate a foreign currency account for ease of administration and perhaps to take advantage of what may be beneficial overdraft interest rates
- *the Export Credits Guarantee Department* (ECGD) can assist overseas traders in two main ways:
  —by insuring the exporter against the risks (both political and commercial) of not being paid for exports
  —by providing a guarantee to the business' bankers under which finance can be obtained for export trade, often at a favourable rate of interest. Such finance may be as much as 100% of the invoice value.
  The guarantee is UK government backed and will normally be for a maximum term of two years, although this period can be extended for such situations as the sale of capital goods, for instance
- *produce loans* In certain circumstances where goods are imported, up to 75–80% of the value of these goods may be made available by a bank. The bank takes security over the goods that are either in a warehouse or in transit. This facility is of great benefit to an importer needing to bridge the gap between paying for the goods and ultimately selling them
- *bills of exchange* Traditionally these have played a major role in the conduct of international trade. Effectively, a bill is an unconditional order in writing, addressed by one person to another, requiring the addressee to pay on demand a certain sum on a given date to a specified person or bearer. If the bill arises as a result of trade it is known as a 'trade bill'.
  Under this mechanism an exporter can draw a bill on an importer and there are two advantages:

—the importer accepting the bill obtains a period of credit in accordance with the terms of the bill, and

—the exporter gets an immediate cash receipt by discounting the bill at a bank.

The cash receipt is discounted by the interest cost for the period of credit and at the end of that period the bank will seek payment of the bill from the importer. Clearly, there is some risk to be evaluated in respect of the credit status of the importer and generally there is a contingent liability to the exporter, because the bank will have a right of recourse against the drawer for non-payment by the importer.

A bill of exchange is a negotiable instrument which can be traded in the financial markets depending on the status of the various parties to the transactions

- *documentary letters of credit*   This is one of the most common methods used to ensure payment by overseas customers. Typically, a letter of credit will be issued by a bank in the importer's country and confirmed by a bank in the UK. Once confirmed, the UK bank will accept bills of exchange against presentation of the required documentation. This enables rapid payment to be made to the exporter at a relatively modest cost

- *forward contracts*   A forward exchange contract is an agreement to purchase or sell one foreign currency for another at a future date. They are generally used by trading companies to hedge against purchase or sale commitments that they enter into and which are denominated in foreign currencies. In addition, however, they can be used in treasury management as shown by the following illustration:

1/7/89		31/12/89
Need £10m	UK average rate of interest 10%	repay £10m

US average rate of interest 6%

Company A borrows £10 million for six months from 1 July 1989 to 31 December 1989. The UK interest rate is 10%, but the company is aware that if it borrows US Dollars, the interest rate is currently 6%.

Therefore, Company A borrows $17.5 million and converts it at prevailing exchange rates to £10 million. At the same time Company A enters into a forward contract to sell, say £10.1 million in six months time for $17.5 million to repay the US loan. During the term of the loan, interest is paid on the US dollar borrowing at the rate of 6%.

Result:
Borrow $17.5 million @$1.750 = £1   £10m
Sell £10.1 million forward @
    forward rate of, say, $1.732 = £1 $17.5m

	£'000
US interest cost for six months	300
Exchange loss	100
	400
UK interest cost for six months	500
Saving	100

- *parallel loans* These first became popular when exchange controls restricted companies' overseas funding. They are now used as a means of funding subsidiaries overseas. The basic mechanism is for a company in the UK needing funds abroad to swap funds with a foreign company needing funds in the UK. Banks will often act as intermediaries in these agreements. Similarly, currency swaps are a development of the parallel loan whereby the parties sell each other currencies. These agreements tend to be for the longer-term and generally involve the currencies being repaid at the end of the swap period at their original exchange price.

Working capital management

The sources of finance discussed so far have concentrated on the availability of external finance. Equally important to the financing of growth is the effective management of the company's existing resources. Lack of effective control in this area is one of the most common causes of business failure, and the casualty rate for smaller businesses in their formative years is particularly high, since there may be a lack of cumulative reserves and cash resources to meet adverse or fluctuating circumstances. Whilst no business can completely insure itself against the unexpected, the effects of a downturn in trade can be minimised by sound cash and working capital management. A wide variety of techniques can be employed and the most important are briefly summarised below:

1. *credit policy for debtors* In most trading situations credit will be granted to customers, as it is likely that a cash on delivery policy would greatly impede sales volume growth. Management should ensure that the financial position and reputation of all customers is carefully evaluated prior to the granting of credit, by a combination of such steps as:
   - bank references
   - trade references from other suppliers
   - a report from a credit agency (eg Dun & Bradstreet)
   - an analysis of the customers' financial statements, copies of which can be obtained from Companies House
   - personal opinions from meetings, visits to premises etc.
   Any credit control system should include a periodic review of customers' accounts to ensure that pre-set limits are not exceeded. The granting of special terms, which can pressurise a small business wishing to expand sales, must be carefully considered in terms of profitability, cashflow and the effect on other customers

2. *collection policy* Regardless of the agreed terms of trade, there is a prevalent tendency for many companies to withhold payment until they

have been repeatedly reminded and even threatened with legal action. An effective collection policy will enable management to be aware of the age of a debt and to apply an appropriate procedure for collection. Key elements of such a policy might be as follows:

- prompt, accurate aged analysis information which allows potential bad debts to be identified at the earliest stage
- invoicing as early as possible, and no later than date of despatch
- issuing reminders promptly and regularly, with a steadily increasing level of insistence
- refusing follow-on sales until earlier outstanding items have been cleared
- granting settlement discounts for prompt payment of invoices.

The effectiveness of any credit policy will depend ultimately on whether receivables are continuously and persistently followed up

3. *delaying disbursements*   With disbursements, the business is at the converse end of the finance chain. In this instance, the overriding principle is to delay payment rather than expedite it, but the business must be careful to avoid two possible setbacks:

- loss of discount which might outweigh the advantages of delaying settlement
- loss of supplier goodwill and the breakdown of the trading relationship.

Advantage should be taken of any instalment options, providing that interest rates are comparatively favourable to those being paid on other borrowings within the business

4. *short-term investment*   The productive use of surplus cash is a further essential function of working capital and cash management. A substantial number of short-term cash investment possibilities exist and many instruments will mature in as little as one day, such as overnight deposits. Other commonly used investments include money market funds, certificates of deposit and short-term gilts. The key to maximising the return to the business is to review all options before investing. Yields, even on similar instruments, do vary considerably.

Any investment activity should be clearly linked with the cashflow forecasts so that a schedule of maturity can be established which is designed to provide the business with available cash as and when the forecast indicates it will be required. In addition, a margin of error should be allowed, since to borrow money would result in incurring higher interest rates than those being generated on sums invested

5. *stock controls*   Maintaining the appropriate level of inventory is a critical working capital management control. Few businesses can produce entirely to order, and when this is combined with a customer expectation of rapid delivery, the pressure on management to build up stock can be considerable.

The appropriate level of stocks held depends on many factors such as rate of stock turnover, reordering time, and purchase price per unit for varying quantities. Every business will probably have its own special factors impacting upon stock levels. As a general guide, however, the following conditions could be indicative of stock control problems which will need to be urgently addressed:

- stock levels are rising relative to sales

- stock turnover rates are generally below the average for the industry
- poor stock purchasing controls are in place leading to unnecessary build ups
- physical stock counts reveal significant discrepancies compared with stock records
- frequent customer complaints about back orders and missed deliveries
- write-offs for obsolescent or returned stocks are increasing proportionately faster than are overall stock levels.

Generally speaking, to avoid either overstocking or understocking a continuous inventory control is necessary. This can take many different forms, such as regular physical counts, constant evaluation of gross margin etc. The main consideration for any company is to ensure that it has the information and feedback system in place to be able to identify problems at an early stage and rectify them immediately. Stock control is discussed further in Chapter 6, Operations Management.

Conclusion

A wide range of funding sources is available to the management of a growing company. Management must choose the most efficient and economic funding strategy to enable the business to achieve its overall corporate plan. Internal working capital management is as important as seeking finance from outside.

The external sources of finance discussed in this chapter range from conventional bank borrowing through to public flotation. Some guidance has been given on the most appropriate source which should be determined by the needs of the business. Conventional borrowing is normally secured against assets and/or guarantees. However, the secured lender will need to be assured also that the business is viable and its management has developed a plan to enable the company to repay its borrowings and interest as they fall due. The unsecured financier, such as a venture capitalist, is even more dependent upon the quality of the business and its management team, and will seek evidence that the business is well managed and that the growth plans are realistic.

Two aspects that will be particularly scrutinised are:

1. how the company is to achieve its envisaged growth and
2. how the company manages its resources.

Marketing will inevitably play an important role in the achievement of the company's growth plans and this topic is discussed further in Chapter 5, while Chapters 6 and 7 give consideration to the management of operations and human resources.

CHAPTER 4

Taxation Considerations

Introduction

During the 1980s significant changes were seen in the United Kingdom taxation system whereby, for example, individuals are now taxed on income and capital gains at the same rates and we now have relatively (compared to previous periods) low personal and corporate tax rates. Despite these changes there do still remain numerous opportunities for tax planning for both companies and their entrepreneurial management teams.

The growing company, its management and owners may be particularly well positioned to take advantage of tax planning opportunities, but at the same time they must be alert to the numerous tax pitfalls that await the unwary or poorly advised.

Typically, the growing company and its shareholders may need to give careful consideration to the following areas:

Tax planning for the shareholder

Shareholders can take advantage of opportunities in saving capital taxation that may arise following the successful growth of a company. If steps are taken at an early stage the impact of capital taxation may be successfully reduced.

Tax planning for the company

Whilst commercial and operational matters should not be dominated by tax planning, tax should nevertheless be regarded like any other cost that can be controlled. Careful and regular review of the company's activities, both current and proposed, should ensure that the 'tax overhead' is minimised. Indeed, the company's strategy should consider the impact of taxation on its plans for growth.

Tax planning for acquisitions

Many growing companies will, at various stages of their development, sustain growth and profitability through corporate acquisitions. In this event, there are numerous tax planning considerations that should be taken into account, as well as pitfalls to be avoided. The growing company must consider both the tax implications of the acquisition itself and its impact on the group structure thereafter.

Remuneration planning for key employees

Growth, as stressed throughout this book, must be managed. The majority of successful companies are those that have developed their management team as the company has grown. To attract and retain the key members of the management team, senior personnel must be adequately rewarded. During the 1980s attention was focused on the development of the remuneration package for key members of the management team. In particular, the share option or share incentive scheme has been an important element of many senior remuneration packages. Use of share option schemes, where unquoted share values are negotiable, or deferred bonus schemes provide a significant capital or income reward for the executive, in addition to the normal salary, pensions and benefits package that is provided.

Summary

The fundamental discipline to be followed is that planning should always be undertaken at the earliest opportunity and reviewed regularly thereafter if that planning is to secure benefits for the company, its shareholders and its executives.

This chapter, which states current law and practice as we understand it, is intended to assist the growing company in identifying the areas which may benefit from a careful review from a tax viewpoint. It is not intended as a comprehensive tax planning guide but merely as an aid in identifying areas with planning potential.

No publication can ever provide an effective substitute for professional advice. The application of this chapter to particular situations will depend on the circumstances involved. It is recommended, therefore, that specific advice is sought before any action is taken.

Tax planning for the shareholder

Introduction

Shareholders should consider two primary elements of tax planning.

Firstly, the shareholder should ensure that the means of reducing the impact of capital taxes has been fully considered. In particular, he should be aware of possible savings in capital gains tax and inheritance tax that may arise after a sale of those shares following a Stock Exchange transaction or listing, or alternatively by a 'trade sale' of the company.

Secondly, it is important that the proceeds from such realisations are invested in a tax efficient manner, having taken into account personal requirements, including the acceptable level of risk to the investor.

Capital tax planning

Capital tax planning should be undertaken at an early stage, so as to take advantage of the relatively low capital value of the company's shares prior to the growth that is anticipated.

Capital gains tax planning

Clearly, individuals seeking to reduce their capital gains tax liability should concentrate their tax planning on those assets likely to appreciate in value. Private company shares are likely to be significant in this context and shareholders who have received advice at an early stage may be able to achieve very considerable deferral or mitigation of gains.

For example, a gift of unquoted shares in a trading company to members of the family who, or certain trusts which, are resident in the UK can be made for 'no gain/no loss'. The new owner inherits the original base cost of the shares against future disposal proceeds.

Particular use can be made of family trusts which are resident offshore. Such trusts do not suffer UK capital gains tax on disposals and therefore they are generally located in countries where there is no local tax either (such as Jersey or Guernsey). Transfer of unquoted shares at an early stage into such areas as trusts can provide for substantial tax free capital appreciation, until a benefit is made available to a UK resident, although care must be taken not to incur extra income tax liabilities.

Where some growth in share value has already occurred, then it is possible to secure the benefits of offshore status in the future by use of a UK trust in the first instance. Where the transfer into the UK trust qualifies as a 'no gain/no loss', the tax cost of a subsequent move offshore is the amount of this frozen liability.

Inheritance tax planning

On death the value of the shares will form part of the estate of the proprietor. Specialist tax valuers would seek to negotiate low values for unquoted shares with Shares Valuation Division of the Inland Revenue. In addition, business property relief may well be available to reduce the value further. The first £128,000 of value in the estate does not carry a tax charge but this does not usually cover more than the family home; above that the tax rate is 40%.

In contrast, lifetime gifts are charged to tax at 20%, once again after the £128,000 threshold has been used. More important, however, is the fact that most lifetime gifts are *potentially exempt* from *tax* (PET's) if the donor survives seven years.

Clearly, the future lifespan of the donor is not known at the time when the gift is made and so protective measures must be considered. The most important is to make gifts at an early stage when low values may be attributed to the shares. Where this is not possible consider:

- the availability of 'taper relief' for shares gifted at least three years before death
- the availability of 'business property relief' if the shares remain unquoted, ie not quoted on the International Stock Exchange list nor the Unlisted Securities Market, or the holding is a majority holding
- insurance to cover the tax. Obviously, if the donor is in a high risk insurance category the premiums may be so high as to render this option uneconomic.

Significant inheritance tax savings may also be achieved if shares are settled on discretionary trusts. This is because the capital appreciation, arising from a subsequent flotation or sale of the company's shares, will belong to the settlement and not form part of the settlor's estate for inheritance tax purposes. One potential cost of discretionary trusts is that the value of the property included in the trust is assessed to inheritance tax on every tenth anniversary of its creation. It may be possible to avoid this charge, however, by winding up the settlement or creating an 'interest in possession' (such that someone, other than the settlor, has a right to the trust income) or an accumulation and maintenance settlement (for children or grandchildren aged under 25) within the first ten years of the trust.

Commercial considerations

As with all tax planning, the shareholders should consider the commercial implications of their planning. Here there are two main considerations. Firstly, the donor should ensure the gift does not deprive him and his spouse of a reasonable living standard both presently and in the future, and secondly, that the donee does not misuse the income and capital that he will derive from the gift. The latter concern is normally protected by the use of trusts.

Tax efficient investment

Shareholders who have realised a significant capital sum from the sale of their shares should give consideration to investing part of those funds in investments which provide an element of tax relief against their income. Examples of these include:

PENSIONS

Here the entrepreneur should consider the payment of premiums into a personal pension scheme, or additional voluntary contributions to a company scheme, to obtain the maximum pension entitlement and tax-free lump sum on retirement, assuming that the scheme is not already fully funded. (Professional advice should be sought to determine the amount of premium payments to be made, as the maximum will depend upon specific circumstances.)

UNQUOTED SHARES

Where the individual has made an investment in an unquoted company and that investment has not attracted any tax relief under BES (see below) and a loss has been made, then he should consider claiming the capital loss arising as an income tax deduction rather than a capital gains tax loss.

BUSINESS EXPANSION SCHEME (BES)

Providing specific conditions are met, UK resident tax payers can claim income tax relief, at their highest rates of tax, on investments of up to

£40,000 per annum in certain unquoted UK companies. From 6 April 1990 both husband and wife are each entitled to a £40,000 relief from such an investment. However, investors should be aware that to retain the income tax relief they will need to retain the shares for a period of five years. They should also not overlook the commercial risk attaching to any investment opportunity. BES investments have to be made in either unquoted trading companies or companies letting property under assured tenancies and inevitably carry a high degree of risk.

BUILDINGS IN ENTERPRISE ZONES

An investment made, either directly or through a managed property invest-ment trust, in an industrial or commercial building sited in an Enterprise Zone will obtain a 100% initial allowance on the amount of the expenditure attributed to the building (but not the land) and this may be set against the investor's taxable income.

There is no limit to such investments or to the income tax relief. To avoid a clawback of relief this should generally be viewed as a 25 year investment, although in certain circumstances it is possible to recover part of the capital investment at an earlier date without loss of the tax relief.

INTEREST RELIEF

In addition, in respect of certain holdings in unquoted shares (other than those on which BES relief is claimed) and expenditure on buildings in Enterprise Zones, individuals may wish to use borrowings to finance their investment. Borrowings for such investments will enable the investor to claim income tax relief on the interest paid.

GOVERNMENT SECURITIES AND CORPORATE BONDS

Individuals may also consider an investment in government securities and corporate bonds. Since 2 July 1986, all disposals of such investments or options or futures in either of these are exempt from capital gains tax, although accrued income included in the sale proceeds may be subject to income tax. The ability to claim capital losses in certain situations has now been rectified by the Budget of March 1990.

Tax planning for the company

Introduction

It is important that a company's taxation situation, and the taxation impli-cations of any significant proposed transactions, are reviewed regularly. In particular, a review should be conducted prior to the financial year-end based on reliable management accounts and forecasts. This review should take place sufficiently in advance of the year-end so that any necessary transactions may be considered to mitigate tax liabilities arising in the current accounting period.

In addition, this review can be used to ensure that all necessary claims and elections have been lodged within the time limits as set down in legislation.

Again, the review of the company's tax affairs should take into account the overall commercial requirements. Care should be taken to recognise the impact of tax planning on cash flow and profitability, particularly for those companies seeking to establish or maintain a growth 'track record'.

A number of tax planning initiatives and reviews which are relevant to the growing company are outlined below.

Deferral of taxable profits

A company's taxable profits may be deferred by:

- deferring income; for example, by deferring the sale of goods or services to a later accounting period, or by changing the length of an accounting period to enable a loss of a later period to be included, or to enable profits of a later period to be assessed at a later date. Clearly any deferral of income must not over-ride acceptable accounting practice
- increasing the capital allowances immediately available; for example, by advancing the date on which expenditure is incurred on assets qualifying for capital allowances or by bringing forward the date of asset disposals so as to establish a balancing allowance. In addition, a review of capital expenditure may show whether scientific research allowances, at 100%, could be claimed instead of plant and machinery allowances (25% writing down allowances) or industrial buildings allowances (4% writing down allowances). Accelerating allowances in this way would clearly reduce tax liabilities and benefit cash flow
- advancing revenue expenditure; this may be achieved, for example, by accelerating bonus payments to directors, making additional pension contributions, accelerating interest and other payments which rank as a charge on income and making specific provision for such items as bad debts, obsolete stocks and redundancy costs. As for all other expenditure, the amount and timing of such costs should be based on bona fide transactions, as well as having commercial logic.

Utilisation of trading losses

Consideration should be given to the following:

- utilising any current trading losses, by way of a carry back to the previous accounting period where they may be offset against earlier taxable profits
- utilising surplus trading losses to obtain a repayment of tax credits related to franked investment income (dividends from UK companies)

- by ensuring, where possible, that chargeable gains on the sale of assets are made in the same accounting period as losses are incurred and prior to any cessation of trade.

Creation of losses by way of new investment

If commercially justifiable, a company may be in a position whereby trading losses are created from a new investment. That investment might comprise an investment in a new trading venture, which in its early stage incurs trading losses as a result of start-up costs, including expenditure on assets qualifying for capital allowances or an investment in a building in an Enterprise Zone giving rise to a 100% initial allowance.

Timing of asset disposals

If a significant chargeable gain is likely to arise from disposal of a 'qualifying asset' (including buildings, land, fixed plant or machinery and goodwill) that is used in the company's trade, consideration should be given to:

- reinvestment of the proceeds from such a sale in new qualifying assets, in the period 12 months preceding or three years following the disposal so as to defer the chargeable gain arising for at least ten years and perhaps indefinitely ('roll over')
- deferring the sale of the asset until a subsequent accounting period, so as to delay the taxation arising
- realising the gain in the same accounting period that trading losses or charges on income are available for offset
- transferring the asset to another group company which has capital losses to reduce or eliminate the gain.

Reviewing a group structure

The tax position of the whole group should be regularly reviewed so as to ensure:

- the most beneficial group relief position is achieved (see page 87)
- that any Advance Corporation Tax (ACT) paid by the group is used in the most beneficial manner
- that tax due on chargeable gains is minimised, either by the use of capital losses in the group, or the roll-over of any gains against qualifying expenditure within the group

- that the number of trading companies in the group is reduced so as to maximise the use of the lower rates of corporation tax (at 25% rather than 35%)
- that inter company trading does not create tax liabilities on unrealised profits
- that all claims and elections are complete and submitted on time.

Reviewing the timing and amount of dividend payments to shareholders

If dividend payments to shareholders are intended, consideration should be given to ensure that ACT is used at the earliest opportunity and in the best manner, and is paid as late as possible.

The following matters should be taken into account:

- the availability of franked investment income, and associated tax credit, which reduces the level of ACT payable
- the availability of taxable income and Mainstream Corporation Tax against which the ACT may be offset, either in respect of the accounting period in which the dividend is paid or accounting periods in the previous six years
- the payment of dividends immediately before the company's financial year-end so as to minimise the period between payment of the ACT and the date when it may be used to reduce the company's Mainstream Corporation Tax liability
- the payment of dividends early in a return period (ACT is accounted for on a quarterly basis) so as to maximise the interval between the date of the dividend payment and the due date for the payment of the related ACT
- the impact of changes in the basic rate of income tax. For example, a reduction in the basic rate of income tax in the next fiscal year may justify the deferral of a dividend payment until after 5 April, whereas an increase in the basic rate of income tax may warrant the payment of dividends being brought forward before 6 April.

Any dividend policy must also consider the impact upon the shareholders. For instance, the bringing forward of a dividend may increase the level of taxable income of the shareholders in a tax year when rates are higher.

Finally, there has been a trend amongst private companies to pay dividends rather than director's remuneration, primarily to avoid employer's national insurance contributions. This saving of national insurance may have the following adverse results:

- cash flow or interest costs in funding additional ACT arising on the increased level of dividend payments
- reduced pension entitlements for directors as a result of lower remuneration levels
- higher valuations of the company's shares for capital gains tax or inheritance tax purposes.

Consideration of international tax aspects

As a company grows it may establish overseas operations. The following should then be considered:

- whether those operations should be conducted through a branch or company structure. Generally a new venture, which initially incurs losses, should be conducted through a branch so as to enable those losses to be offset against UK taxable profits. Once that activity becomes profitable the branch can be incorporated so that profits will not be taxed until they are remitted to the UK by way of dividend. A Capital Gains Tax liability could arise on the transfer of the overseas assets from a branch to an overseas resident subsidiary. Such assets include goodwill which may be attributed a value by the Revenue upon incorporation of the branch. However the 1990 Budget promises a much needed change to remove this potential worry
- the level of overseas tax suffered, both on trading profits arising overseas and as a withholding tax on dividends remitted to the UK, and whether these overseas taxes can be fully offset against UK tax liabilities on the dividend
- the terms of trade between the UK company and its overseas subsidiary. The concern here is that the Inland Revenue has powers to adjust the profits of the UK company if its transactions with the overseas company are deemed not to be carried out on an 'arm's length' basis. Likewise many other countries have similar laws so there is potential for extra expense
- an overseas subsidiary may be 'thinly capitalised' (high level of borrowing from a UK holding company as compared to the equity funding) so that the interest charges would be higher than that normally available on a third party basis. The local revenue authorities would then impute a lower figure for interest paid (and less of an expense to be set against profits therefore) so that the balance is treated as a dividend
- the impact of the legislation on 'controlled foreign companies' and in certain cases whether the overseas company follows an acceptable distribution policy to avoid the whole of its profits being assessed to UK tax
- the impact of exchange gains and losses and their tax treatment in the UK.

Reviewing PAYE and related matters

As growth continues it is inevitable that the personnel resource will increase to support the expansion of the company. This can lead to compliance problems with PAYE regulations and reporting requirements. New problems may be encountered for the first time.

Over recent years compliance with PAYE regulations and P11D reporting requirements has become highly relevant to employers. The Revenue's compliance units have been successful in collecting substantial amounts of tax (and interest and penalties) for prior years. Some of the issues that are raised can be negotiated without too much difficulty, but many are more complex and give rise to significant differences of opinion. Consequently, it is recommended that professional advice is sought from an expert in PAYE compliance matters.

The professional advisor can assist an employer in the following circumstances:

1. He can carry out a review of an employer's procedures, to identify any areas of non-compliance or doubt and give advice on the action that

should be taken. Where a review has identified areas of non-compliance, it will normally be appropriate to make a voluntary disclosure to the Revenue. The manner in which the disclosure is made is all important, but it is generally reflected in the negotiated settlement and any penalties would be avoided or at least mitigated to the maximum extent.

2. He can give ad hoc advice on specific issues arising. Where the issue is one in which the interpretation of the legislation is unclear, it may be appropriate to discuss this with the Inspector of Taxes if the amounts involved are material.

   The following is a list of some of the issues where non-compliance may result in a material exposure and where advice should be sought:

   - casual labour payments
   - home to office travel payments
   - round sum allowances
   - overseas travel involving spouses of employees
   - working rule agreements in particular industries
   - travel and subsistence payments to employees who spend significant time working at clients' offices
   - living accommodation available for employees
   - incentive awards and payments.

3. Advice can also be given in relation to dispensations from reporting specified payments on employees' P11Ds. When dispensations are issued, the Inspector will have requested that any changes in the circumstances are advised to him, for example an increase in the amount of a round sum allowance. If changes have not been notified, then the dispensation may have technically lapsed. It is important to review the changed circumstances and to take steps to renegotiate the dispensation and deal with any matters arising. Requests for a dispensation, where one has not previously been obtained, may lead to a P11D compliance review by the Revenue. Here it is important that payments made and benefits provided, together with the resulting necessary P11D disclosures, are reviewed in advance of the dispensation request, so that any areas of non-compliance or doubt are identified and considered.

4. Where a claim to tax and national insurance has been made by the Revenue, the employer needs to take account of all available experience in negotiating a settlement. There are many factors that can have an impact on a final settlement, and it is unlikely that any employer acting in isolation will have the appropriate expertise. It is therefore recommended that an advisor is involved, as he can bring to bear experience in dealing with the particular issues raised and skill in negotiating settlements. Initially, the advisor will be able to review the claim and provide a preliminary view as to whether it is appropriate, and indeed cost effective, for his involvement.

   With the introduction of the new penalty regime, the possibility of the imposition of penalties and any arguments in mitigation will be of particular relevance and can also be considered at this initial meeting.

Where penalties are likely to be significant it is recommended that an advisor is involved.

It is beyond the scope of this book to provide an in-depth discussion of PAYE matters, however Appendix C (page 150) provides answers to the most common questions asked by employers with regard to compliance, assessments and other common problems.

Reviewing VAT matters

The 1985 Finance Act introduced severe penalties for failure to comply with VAT regulations. It is important that companies constantly review their VAT compliance procedures so as to ensure that the regulations are adhered to and that any misdeclaration or failure to comply with those regulations is remedied immediately. Appendix D (page 160) discusses the VAT planning considerations of relevance to the growing company.

Tax planning for acquisitions

Introduction

The structure of a purchase or sale of a company or its business assets is influenced predominantly by the taxation implications of the proposed transaction. Both the vendor and the purchaser will have tax concerns. In many instances, the vendor's main tax consideration will be to avoid a sale of the business assets and thereby avoid the consideration for the sale being taxed at more than 40% (the effective rate) first on the sale of the assets by the company and then again when profits are extracted from the company by way of dividend. It is important that the purchaser and vendor resolve the format at the outset.

Even before that, however, the purchaser and his advisors should assess fully the overriding strategic rationale for the acquisition, as this should ultimately determine the overall structure of the acquisition.

Acquisition of a business

As mentioned previously it is more common for a vendor to dispose of a company (ie the shares) rather than a business (ie the assets). This should prevent extra tax liabilities.

However, a purchaser may wish to negotiate the purchase of a business and its assets with a view to obtaining the following benefits:

- the purchaser may obtain a higher level of capital allowances on qualifying assets than would be the case on the assets underlying the acquisition of shares
- the purchaser may be able to 'roll-over' chargeable gains from other transactions into qualifying asset purchases
- the base cost for calculating chargeable gains on future asset sales is likely to be greater than the historic values of those assets within any company which is acquired

- the purchaser avoids any undisclosed liabilities from the past (which can be expensive to resolve).

These benefits may be substantially reduced, in terms of tax savings, where the acquisition of assets gives rise to an increased stamp duty cost, eg where the value of the assets is attributable predominantly to land and buildings bearing stamp duty at 1%, as compared to a rate of 0.5% arising on the transfer of shares in a company (and 0% from 1991/92 as announced in the 1990 Budget).

As noted above, an asset sale may not be acceptable to the vendor. The advantages of an asset purchase for the purchaser are usually matched by disadvantages for the vendor. For instance, higher values attributed to assets could give rise to a clawback of capital allowances and substantial chargeable gains on which corporation tax would be payable by the vendor.

Acquisition of a company

INVESTIGATION OF THE TARGET COMPANY'S HISTORY AND OPERATIONS

Normally, a purchaser will instruct his accountants to carry out an investigation of the target company. The scope of that investigation will depend upon a number of factors, including the purchaser's own ability to carry out a sufficient review in the time available (if the acquisition is to be completed to a short timetable) and, above all, the level of reliance that can be placed on the warranties and indemnities, given by the vendor and contained in the purchase and sale agreement (see below).

It would be usual to carry out a review of the company's financial history and its financial and accounting controls (see Chapter 8). In addition, the review would cover the main taxation aspects of the company's past and present activities. The results of the review are likely to influence the purchaser in negotiating the final price. For instance, the review might establish that the company had failed to provide for deferred taxation in respect of specific timing differences or failed to meet VAT or PAYE requirements. Accordingly, the target company's assets may be overstated and, further, penalties and negotiating costs may be incurred ultimately by the new owner in resolving matters.

THE PURCHASE AND SALE AGREEMENT

The basis on which the purchase is made is normally set out in the purchase and sale agreement. In this agreement, statements will be made by the vendor on which the purchaser will rely in making the acquisition. In doing so the purchaser will require the vendor to warrant that those statements are true. These are the 'warranties' and they are very necessary to protect the purchaser from past tax problems.

These warranties will apply except where the vendor makes disclosures. Those disclosures, normally contained in a 'Disclosure Letter', will seek to limit the vendor's liabilities by disclaiming responsibility or liability for any matter or issue disclosed. The disclosures may well give rise to a variation in the final consideration or, in difficult situations, the transaction may not proceed.

In addition, the purchaser will require a deed of tax indemnity from the vendor. The purpose of this indemnity is to provide the purchaser with a means of recovering tax liabilities not provided for or agreed as disclosed at the time of purchase.

In agreeing the warranty and indemnity provisions in the purchase and sale agreement, it will be necessary to establish the following:

- the maximum liability to be assumed by the vendor
- the minimum liability which the purchaser must prove he has incurred before any claims can be made
- the period subsequent to the completion of the purchase within which claims must be submitted so as to be valid.

In making a claim the purchaser should have the following recourse:

- an action for breach of warranty
- a right to indemnity under the deed of indemnity
- a right to rescind the agreement (for example upon a discovery of material differences from the matters contained in the warranties or the letter of disclosure).

The tax warranties are normally separately identified in the purchase and sale agreement and will normally be listed in extensive detail under the following headings:

- general tax warranties
- corporation tax
- stamp duty
- capital duty
- value added tax
- development land tax
- inheritance tax, capital transfer tax and estate duty
- PAYE
- national insurance contributions
- close company considerations
- anti-avoidance provisions
- other taxes.

THE CONSIDERATION FOR THE ACQUISITION OF A COMPANY

The consideration provided by the purchaser for the acquisition of a company can take a number of forms, including:

- cash; or
- shares; or
- loan stock; or
- a mixture of cash, shares or loan stock.

Cash will often be the basis of the consideration, especially if the purchaser's shares are not publicly traded.

Alternatively, both purchaser and vendor may wish to settle the consideration by an issue of shares in the purchaser. For the purchaser, this will avoid a reduction in cash resources or an increase in borrowings; for the vendor it should mean a postponement of the capital gain (as he should be able to 'hold-over' the gain until he sells the new shares). In accepting a shares alternative, the vendor will consider the income yield on those shares and the likelihood of capital appreciation.

A further alternative for the purchaser and vendor, may be to settle the consideration by way of an issue of loan stock in the purchasing company. This alternative enables the vendor to postpone tax, probably obtain a reasonable income yield and receive a fixed capital return. However, most vendors would wish the loan stock to be guaranteed by a bank, particularly where the purchaser is not a substantial established company. Purchasers may be reluctant to provide such a guarantee because of the impact on their accounts.

Further requirements are possible, an example being the use of convertible loan stock at a lower interest cost in exchange for some potential for capital appreciation.

In recent years, purchasers have been increasingly concerned as to the future performance potential of their acquisitions. Accordingly, many transactions have included a consideration based on the future results or growth in asset value of the acquired company. Such an approach has given rise to a particular taxation problem for the vendors in relation to the value and timing of the additional consideration to be received. To some extent, that problem has been overcome following the Inland Revenue's publication of an extra-statutory concession in April 1988. This provides that where the additional consideration takes the form of shares or loan stock, then the charge to tax for that further consideration is postponed until the shares or loan stock are eventually sold for cash.

In the case of vendors who have service agreements with the acquired company, there may be a suggestion that those vendors should receive payment for compensation for loss of office. While this is unlikely to be a benefit to the vendor for compensation paid in excess of £30,000 (as this is likely to be taxed at the same rate as the gain on the sale of shares) the purchaser, in theory, would obtain a corporation tax deduction for the whole compensation sum. However, that deduction is likely to be disallowed if the Inland Revenue considers the payment is not commensurate with the terms of the service agreement, or the purchase consideration has been adjusted for that compensation sum.

OTHER TAX ASPECTS OF ACQUIRING A COMPANY

There are a number of other tax aspects to consider at the time of an acquisition. These include:

Advance tax clearances   There are two principal tax clearances that may be sought from the Inland Revenue in advance of a proposed acquisition:

- from Technical Division (Section 703 Group) that the transaction will not give rise to an income tax liability

- and from Technical Division (Capital Gains under CGTA 1979, section 88) that the exchange of shares or securities will be regarded as deferring the capital gain.

Whilst these clearances are principally for the benefit of the vendor, they will assist the purchaser in that he will be assured that the consideration will be treated as a capital transaction, rather than one with income tax obligations.

Disallowance of trading losses and the loss of surplus ACT   For a number of years there has been tax legislation in place to prevent the purchase of companies for the benefit of their past trading losses or surplus ACT.

The denial of the future use of such trading losses or ACT can apply where:

- within any period of three years there is both a change in the ownership of a company and a major change in the nature or conduct of a trade carried on by the company
  or
- there is a change in the ownership of the company at any time after the scale of the activities in the trade carried on by a company has become small or negligible, and before any considerable revival of the trade.

For these purposes 'major change in the nature or conduct of the trade' is defined as including:

- a major change in the type of property dealt in, or services, or facilities provided in the trade
  or
- a major change in customers, outlets or markets of the trade

and is to apply even if the change is the result of a gradual process which began outside the period of three years mentioned above.

It is clear that a company acquisition, undertaken for commercial reasons, could come within the ambit of this legislation, for example by a rationalisation of the target company's activities. Accordingly, care should be taken if these circumstances could potentially arise.

Crystallisation of chargeable gains upon a takeover   Normally, the acquisition of a company will not have any impact on that company's own tax position. However, purchasers and their advisors need to be aware of the possible impact of ICTA 1970, section 278 where a subsidiary company is purchased.

This section provides that if a company ceases to be a member of a group, corporation tax on chargeable gains is to be paid by that company in respect of any asset acquired from the former group within the six years preceding the takeover.

The measure of the gain is the difference between the cost of that asset to the former group, as compared with market value on the day it was transferred into the relevant subsidiary, with appropriate relief for indexation.

A liability could be substantial. Accordingly, the purchaser and his advisors must make full enquiry to ensure that the provisions do not apply, or if they do, that the consideration for the purchase is amended to take account of the liability.

Group relief planning   The term 'group relief' covers reliefs which one company in a group ('the surrendering company') allows another company in the same group ('the claimant company') to use to reduce its liability to corporation tax. The following are eligible for group relief:

- trading losses
- capital allowances
- excess management expenses
- excess charges on income.

When a company acquires another company or group of companies the following general points need to be considered:

- whether a company qualifies for group relief
- the date the acquired company joins the group
- the amounts eligible for group relief.

Two companies are members of the same group for group relief purposes if one is a 75% subsidiary of the other, or both are 75% subsidiaries of a third company.

When a company's ownership changes one accounting period ends in the old group and a new accounting period commences with the new group. Thereafter, that new accounting period ends when the normal accounting period ends. The losses, or other amounts eligible for relief for the normal accounting period, are apportioned on a time basis as between the deemed accounting periods. Similarly, the total profits of the claimant company are apportioned on a time basis between the deemed accounting periods. However, the time-related basis of apportionment may be replaced by some other method if that other method is more equitable, for example on actual basis for interest received.

Group relief is only available in respect of amounts eligible for relief in respect of 'corresponding accounting periods'. If the accounting periods of the surrendering company and the claimant company are not the same, the amount which can be set off is limited by a formula to that part of the accounting period of each which is common to both.

In addition to the general principles mentioned above, consideration should be given to the impact of double taxation relief, taxation payment dates and the use of ACT relief.

Finally, it is essential that the intended allocation of a company's available reliefs, prior to its acquisition, should be detailed in the purchase and sale agreement to avoid any misunderstanding between purchaser and vendor.

Planning for capital losses   It is not possible to transfer capital losses from one group company to another. However, assets showing gains may be transferred within a tax group, or 75% subsidiaries of the same parent company, on a 'no gain, no loss' basis under ICTA 1970, section 273. This legislation does provide planning opportunities.

In a letter to the Institute of Chartered Accountants, in September 1985, the Inland Revenue indicated that they were unlikely to dispute the use of capital losses in a newly acquired subsidiary company, provided those losses were a relatively insubstantial element in the acquisition. Assuming that condition is met the purchaser could transfer assets which show chargeable gains to such companies prior to sale in order to make a tax saving.

Alternatively, the purchaser may have capital losses within its own group, and be able to transfer assets with gains from a newly acquired subsidiary to an existing subsidiary which has capital losses.

Group income planning   Where UK resident companies are members of a group (as defined below) they may jointly elect to pay intergroup dividends without accounting for ACT on the dividends and to pay intergroup charges on income, such as annual interest, without accounting for income tax on those payments.

For these purposes a group relationship exists where the first company is a 51% subsidiary of a second company or the first and second companies are 51% subsidiaries of a third company.

Clearly, such elections can benefit the group cash flow and should be established as soon as an acquisition has taken place.

Such elections must be made in writing to the Inspector of Taxes and are not effective until three months after their submission to the Inspector, unless he notifies his acceptance of the election prior to the end of that period.

It should be noted that the election can be revoked or suspended by notice in advance in respect of any specified dividend, or interest payment, where for example there is a need to utilise ACT arising in the group.

Remuneration planning for key employees

Introduction

As a company grows it is inevitable that the management team will be strengthened and should perhaps receive further incentives to encourage sustained growth.

In such circumstances, it is essential that management is provided with a competitive remuneration package. That remuneration package is likely to comprise the following:

- salary and bonuses
- benefits, including pension contributions
- share options or share incentive schemes.

In recent years, management teams have been prepared to take a far greater element of their remuneration in a package linked to performance in order to obtain a substantial benefit.

As previously noted, share options and share incentive schemes can be a very attractive element of remuneration packages, particularly where the shares of the company are expected to show significant capital growth over a relatively short time scale.

Types of share option and share incentive scheme available

PURCHASE OF SHARES

The initial consideration, and one that is usually favoured by management, is to provide senior personnel with shares from existing shareholders by way of outright purchase. However, to ensure that there is no tax liability for the personnel acquiring those shares they will need to pay full value for those shares. Another drawback is that the value of that shareholding, particularly where a material stake in the company is acquired, may be beyond the individual's financial capacity.

There are also significant considerations for the vendors of those shares, both in terms of capital gains tax and inheritance tax, where significant reductions in their shareholdings could prejudice future claims to capital gains tax retirement relief or inheritance tax business property relief.

SHARE SCHEMES

Where there are problems with the outright purchase of shares, the parties involved should consider share schemes. There are a number of schemes available and variations can usually apply to 'standard schemes' to suit individual situations. The most common schemes used are 'approved' and 'unapproved' share option schemes. The particular benefit of these schemes is that they can be used for a relatively small number of key employees.

APPROVED SHARE OPTION SCHEMES

Under an approved share option scheme, certain key employees are invited to take options over shares in the company under specific rules agreed with the Inland Revenue. The options which are granted, at not less than market value, as agreed with the Inland Revenue, are exercisable in a period of not earlier than three years and not later than ten years from the date of the grant.

The members of management benefiting from the option may consider that such schemes have disadvantages, including:

- the limitation to holding, at any given time, unexercised options over shares whose value at the date of grant is the higher of £100,000 and four times their PAYE earnings
- in certain 'close' companies (controlled by their directors or five or fewer participators) an individual is restricted to a maximum of 10% of the company's shares
- shares under option may be subject to pre-emption rights which operate to 'claw back' shares when an employee leaves the company.

Nevertheless, the tax position is certain—the individual pays capital gains tax on the sale of the shares and there is no tax charge upon exercise, as arises with unapproved schemes (see below). In addition, in the event of a take-over of the company an employee should be entitled to exercise the options or exchange those options for replacement options granted by the acquiring company, subject to the agreement of the acquiring company.

UNAPPROVED SHARE OPTION SCHEMES

Under an unapproved scheme it is possible to grant an individual an option over the company's shares without obtaining Inland Revenue approval and for the option to be granted over as large a proportion of the company's shares as is desired.

The disadvantage for individuals with such schemes is the timing of tax payments. There may be an income tax liability on the date of exercise and if the option is capable of being exercised more than seven years after the date of grant, and the option is granted with an exercise price below the market value at the date of grant, there could be a further income tax charge as at the date of grant.

EMPLOYEE SHARE OWNERSHIP PLANS

Employee Share Ownership Plans (ESOPS) is a generic term: the meaning depends upon the context in which it is used. In the UK, ESOPS are best thought of as a way in which to provide employees with the opportunity to engage in equity participation (share scheme) arrangements, and as such represent a means to an end (in other words, it is a vehicle for providing share benefits in an approved manner) as opposed to being a stand alone share scheme arrangement. Employees in a private company where there is a limited market for shares may sell their shares to a trust set up under the scheme. The cost is financed by payments from the employing company which should be tax deductible.

The 'qualifying' employee share ownership trust provisions introduced in the Finance Act 1989 are unlikely to prove popular because of their highly restrictive nature. However, 'unqualified' trust arrangements combined with approved or unapproved share schemes (for example, to provide a market for shares in a private company) are enjoying increasing popularity.

BONUS SCHEMES

As mentioned above, increasing numbers of employees are now prepared to take a proportion of their remuneration in the form of performance related bonuses. This has given rise to two types of scheme, profit related pay schemes and deferred remuneration.

Profit related pay

Profit related pay schemes were introduced to encourage the linking of employees' remuneration levels, in part, to the profitability of their business. The incentive provided is that a proportion of the pay should be received free of tax.

For 'profit periods' (a 'profit period' is usually 12 months in length and covers the period in respect of which a particular scheme is running) commencing on or after 1 April 1989, tax relief is available on half of the employee's profit related payments, up to 20% of total pay or £4,000 per year whichever is the lower, ie the maximum tax-free element will be £2,000.

Schemes have to include most of a company's employees and are subject to detailed rules which must be approved by the Inland Revenue. From the commercial viewpoint recent improvements in the tax law mean that they can be self financing.

Deferred remuneration schemes

Deferred remuneration schemes have been established for key executives in many situations. These schemes are intended to be self-financing bonus schemes which generate deferred awards, contingent on individuals remaining in service with the company for a specified period in the future. They are calculated by reference to either a combination of corporate/personal performance criteria or a comparative measure, such as comparing the performance of a company within its market sector.

Income tax is paid by individuals at the time of future payment as income of that year. Similarly a corporation tax deduction will be obtained in the year of payment.

Conclusion

In the current corporate environment, managers are increasingly aware of the different remuneration structures available. Companies and their advisors will need to be aware of these and how to vary the content of the remuneration package for the mutual benefit of those key members of management and the company.

CHAPTER 5

Marketing

Introduction

Sustaining competitive advantage

Growth can seldom be maintained by continuing with the proven and tried formulae of the past. As a company grows it establishes a stronger market presence and more complex internal structures and as a result activities must change to address the revised priorities of this new situation. A number of key changes that must be accommodated are illustrated in Fig 5.1 (pages 94–95).

As the customer and competitive environment evolve, the ground on which competitive battles are fought will change. The growing company must continue to create an advantage over competitors in supplying its goods or services to customers. The source of competitive strength that was responsible for the first phase of growth must be recognised but also effort must be refocused to achieve advantage in the critical new arenas of competition. The three key areas in which this competitive advantage can be sought are in the product, the ability to market it and the costs of producing it.

PRODUCT

The initial source of competitive advantage for the growing company is normally the superior performance of the product itself. The growing company will, at some stage in its development, need to confront one or both of two difficulties in responding to competitive pressure:

1. developing a second and subsequent generation of products
2. building a superior service to counter equality in products.

MARKET ACCESS

Marketing skills become increasingly important as a market grows. These skills may be required either to convince the more reluctant second wave of customers to enter the market or to reassure established customers of the product's superiority. Competitors who have delayed their entry into a market with a relevant product are often larger companies with a wider range of products with which to enhance their position with customers. To provide protection against this the concept of product superiority must be firmly established with customers.

COST

Although it is in the producer's interest to refrain from using the price weapon as long as possible, in a poorly differentiated market, such as petrol retail, the temptation to reduce price becomes increasingly strong. It is important to restrain costs as early as possible in a product's life. This provides protection against a price war and, more constructively, provides the cashflow to develop subsequent generations of product.

Key issues

The marketing issues that should be addressed in a company's growth phase are therefore:

- creating an even flow of growing demand through a broadening product portfolio, a wider customer portfolio, or greater repeat purchases
- harnessing the initial energy and enthusiasm for working towards first orders/gaining distribution, to the more methodical process of managing and stabilising the business
- establishing an effective internal infrastructure which produces information quickly on:
  —customer requests/requirements
  —business performance versus plan
  —competitive performance and
- balancing the spirit of enterprise to create new opportunities with effective management of the established business.

These key issues can be addressed through developing an effective marketing capability within the growing company.

The role of marketing

Marketing is not an extension of sales but is a function that integrates the activities of the company into a profitable development plan. The key factors in this role for the growing company are:

- *product development* Sustaining the competitive edge through well planned and relevant product initiatives
- *service* Introducing the service elements of the marketing mix to develop relationships with established customers
- *positioning* Creating an area of competitive advantage that is relevant to a sector of the market and using that competitive advantage to communicate with customers
- *marketing mix management* Managing product features, price, advertising the sales force, direct mail, etc as an integrated and mutually supportive activity rather than events in isolation
- *sustaining internal communications* Linking the whole organisation to the service of the customer.

Fig 5.1

	NEW BUSINESS PHASE I GROWTH	ESTABLISHED BUSINESS PHASE II GROWTH	TRANSITION FROM I TO II IMPLICATIONS FOR MARKETING ACTION AND STRATEGY
1.	Devotes resources to 'getting' business, ie obtaining first orders, first customers.	Devotes resources primarily to building current business and only secondarily to building new businesses/products.	Single-minded effort of launching products is replaced by a need to respond to more balanced range of business issues; Production—sustaining quality, reducing lead times, managing stock. Marketing—launching subsequent generation products, building service, planned diversification. Distribution—reliability. Finance—cashflow, central pressure on costs.
2.	Goes for first order.	Provides customer service to maintain loyalty/encourage repeat purchase.	
3.	Creating awareness and informing customers.	Sustains awareness and builds product values/reminds consumers.	Introductory advertising announces product presence to target audience. Phase II advertising consolidates product's attributes, emphasises product superiority or point of difference. Brand values or reputation are built.
4.	Grows rapidly.	Grows steadily but at declining rate.	Move away from trial stimulating strategy to loyalty and repeat purchase strategy.
5.	Invests heavily to create business, ie short-term non-profit focus.	Delivers profit.	Pressure to deliver profit will put pressure on marketing budgets, availability of funds to support trade deals and product price. Strategy must balance the requirements for profit with the needs of the market place.
6.	Is heavily orientated towards R & D sales.	Is dependent on solid *marketing* strategy for continued success.	Heavy R & D and sales involvement necessary to get a product off the ground is replaced by business management needs. Companies become reliant on marketing strategy for direction.

Fig 5.1 – *continued*

7.	Concentrates on core products.	Extends range, improves quality/technology.	In the early phases of growth, marketing should be aware of the risks of diversifying too quickly. Core products should be firmly established before diversification takes place.
8.	Identifies opportunity for new product within market place/identifies new market.	Understands customer/consumer response to own product and competitor products. Modifies product.	Conduct product tests to understand product performance versus competitors. Respond to consumer reactions. Understand 'image' of product through research/feedback from customers. Check results against desired product positioning.
9.	Is pro-active in the market place.	Must be pro-active and *reactive* in the market place.	Need to take initiatives must be tempered with ability to react to competitive activity. Managers must, therefore, monitor activity within market place and be flexible enough to respond to competition.
10.	Takes risk/aggressive.	Minimises risk/defensive.	Strategy moves to *protect* current business. Pricing may be used competitively, promotional devices used to stimulate loyalty or second purchase. Advertising as above.
11.	Plans/estimates potential.	Monitors and measures as well as estimates and plans.	Phase I emphasis will not have been on continuous analysis of performance. In Phase II, systems must be introduced to provide (live) performance information. Performance versus budget will be monitored and assessed monthly or quarterly.
12.	Builds trade or distribution relationships on novelty.	Develops in more competitive environment.	Develop trade deal structure based on volume purchased/customer potential. Sales force follow-up orders.
13.	Focuses on initial costs for launch/investment costs.	Cuts manufacturing costs in order to provide financial resource to build business upfront.	Understand structure of in-house costs and obtain reasonable estimates of competitor costs, perhaps through competitive bench-marking exercise. Potential (i) to cut price; (ii) to increase marketing or trade spend.

Product development

Product development is essential if the growing company is to continue to prosper. The company must focus this development on areas that are relevant to the customer. Many companies achieve their initial success on the basis of product or technological superiority. The initial success is often achieved through an inward focus on a problem that has been identified in existing products in the market. To sustain this success requires a greater focus on the customers whose needs and priorities will change as they become more accustomed to using the product.

Marketing has an important role to play in product development since it is focused on understanding the customer. Product development should switch from being a purely R & D function to one that involves a more co-operative effort between R & D and marketing. This co-operation will need to be managed effectively, as a successful R & D department will inevitably resent the encroachment of 'inexperienced' and 'poorly informed' marketing people upon their areas of expertise.

There are a number of pitfalls in product development facing the growing company:

- continued minor modifications to the product which are seen as irrelevant by the majority of customers and which serve only to confuse them and cost the company dearly in terms of both direct costs and market credibility
- driving a wedge between the research department and its customers. It is vital that development staff see and understand how their products are used by customers so that development effort is focused on the areas that are relevant
- failure to switch effort to the service element of products in sufficient time to avoid the impact of declining product advantage.

Developing and launching new products is expensive. In many markets the cost of developing and marketing new products is the most important component of fixed cost over a product's life. Large corporations may recoup this investment over high sales volumes and are also more able to withstand the financial impact of errors. The smaller company must, therefore, ensure that its development effort is clearly related to thoroughly researched customer needs so as to avoid mis-use of financial and management resources.

Smaller companies must also minimise the unavoidable costs of new product launches. Launching these under an 'umbrella' brand name is one means of reducing the cost of a launch by providing a point of similarity for the customer.

'Weightwatchers' from Heinz provides a good example of this. The Weightwatchers concept is used as an umbrella under which to introduce a stream of new products, building presence across virtually all sectors of the food market: frozen, chilled, canned and bottled. The range is developed from the central core of Heinz business, ie canned, bottled, and expanded into new market areas. All new products introduced were advertised with heavily branded advertising which, at the same time, reinforced the concept for the existing range.

Continuous product initiatives are required, more by some markets than others: eg technology-based products (electronics) and fashion-based products. Regular product initiatives are vital for success in these markets.

Product innovation carries risks which require careful marketing management if such assets are to be minimised. New products can reduce sales from the existing product range rather than those of competitors, thereby suppressing the overall business unnecessarily. Careful analysis of customer requirements is necessary to avoid a 'range extension' product from taking excessive business from existing products.

Successful product management is time consuming. It is therefore more efficient to concentrate effort on a few significant opportunities that have been well researched, rather than attempt to respond to many conflicting demands.

Service

In many markets, the battle for supremacy has shifted from product superiority and into improved customer service. In practice this is often difficult to achieve as the change requires a fundamental shift in company culture.

The areas where a service advantage can be achieved are illustrated in Fig 5. 2 (page 98). The relevance of these areas to any particular market should be investigated through a thorough, yet inherently simple programme of customer research.

A number of points need to be made. Achieving advantage in any service area will take commitment. It requires a redirection of resources from fundamental technical or product research into manufacturing systems, distribution structures and, most importantly, investment in people.

For investment in infrastructure or systems to be recouped, the company's culture must be re-oriented towards customer service. As was stated previously, the marketing task is not one that can be discharged merely by establishing a marketing department. It must involve the whole company in examining and understanding what the customer requires. This frequently involves a radical re-orientation, from a very inward looking resolution of 'problems', to getting the technology to work and to getting the goods out of the factory.

The service element plays an increasingly important role in building consumer loyalty as a company and its markets mature. Good service creates goodwill and this is the essence of brand loyalty. This will assist in generating repeat business and encourage trial through positive customer referral. It will also aid recovery if a competitor is first to the next product innovation.

Fig 5.2: Service Advantages

PRODUCT SUPPORT
Guarantee
Installation
Customisation
Helpline

CUSTOMER CARE
Sales Force
Telephonists
Invoicing
Engineers

LOGISTICS
Stockholding
Just In Time (JIT)
Delivery Performance
Quality Management

Positioning

Creating in the customer a clear understanding of, and belief in, the specific attractions of the product is critical to achieving long run success. Positioning is the term used for analysing the area of most relevant advantage over competitors in a way that may be communicated strongly to customers.

A crucial decision for the growing company is whether to base the communication of your competitive advantage upon a specific product, a product range or the company name. In general, the broader the platform the better, as this is less costly to implement than a narrow, product-based focus. It also provides a ready made platform for launching new products, which can then inherit elements of the reputation of established products.

A totally new identity for a new product is normally only appropriate if it is a significant diversification and depends on different performance criteria for its success.

Having decided upon the basis of competitive advantage, for maximum impact this has to be clearly communicated to customers. That communication and the foundations on which it is based should be:

- relevant to customers' needs
- strong in impact
- credible in delivery
- sustainable.

Too many positionings are based on generic product features rather than real areas of advantage. Customers' needs and their understanding of the relative advantages of competing offerings must be well researched, so that management comprehends the factors which are pivotal to customers' buying decisions. Obviously (but not always adhered to) management has to be scrupulous in ensuring that the company delivers the claimed advantage.

The factors on which the positioning may be based include:

- innovation
- price advantage
- product quality
- brand values
- superior technology.

Innovation   Even where real 'leads' may be small, it can be advantageous to establish a favourable market impression as an 'innovator' or leader. In commodity markets, customers respect the leader, as opposed to the follower, and this favourable impression is sustained beyond the point where any real advantage remains. This is particularly true where strong support is required from distributors or other intermediaries. Examples of this, as a technique for stimulating continued growth, can be provided by most established manufacturers of branded consumer goods, eg Procter and Gamble and Unilever's struggle to introduce the first liquid detergent.

Price advantage   A platform founded solely on price is frequently unsuccessful. To many customers, low price equates to low value. This ensures it is difficult to launch added value products subsequently as a means of enhancing margins. Early containment of costs is required to provide the freedom to respond to price pressures. A more effective platform is 'value in use', where the advantage of the product is the cash it saves customers over competing offerings. This cost saving can often be supported while retaining premium pricing.

As an example, branded manufacturers of consumer goods have suffered as supermarket own-label products compete on price. Whilst branded manufacturers do not charge a lower price, low costs enable them to invest in advertising. Own-label has a 'natural' cost advantage due to lack of marketing expenditure.

Product quality   Superior product quality is a robust defence of competitive advantage. However, quality has to be seen from the perspective of the customers. Their rating of product features may not match that of the company's technicians. Careful company research may be required to establish what quality actually means. Product maps such as that illustrated in Fig 5.3 (page 100) may be helpful in determining relevant values for communication to customers. In many instances the advantage may be marginal. Strong communication can, however, reinforce apparently relatively minor advantages. 'There's no taste like Heinz', 'Persil washes whiter', 'Only the crumbliest, flakiest chocolate ...' (Cadbury), provide examples for a 'minor' product advantage that has been built into significance through being the major differentiation between competing products.

Brand values   Brand values are used to build emotive responses to a product; these influence consumer purchase for reasons other than logic or rationale. The most effective brand values are significant in the context of the product's market sector:

- safety reassurance for baby products (brands can be rapidly eroded if this is destroyed, eg glass in baby foods)
- forefront of technology: Philips 'simply years ahead'
- safety and reliability: Volvo cars
- image projection: Christian Dior, Yves St Laurent.

Fig 5.3: Positioning Map

Example - Hi-fi Equipment

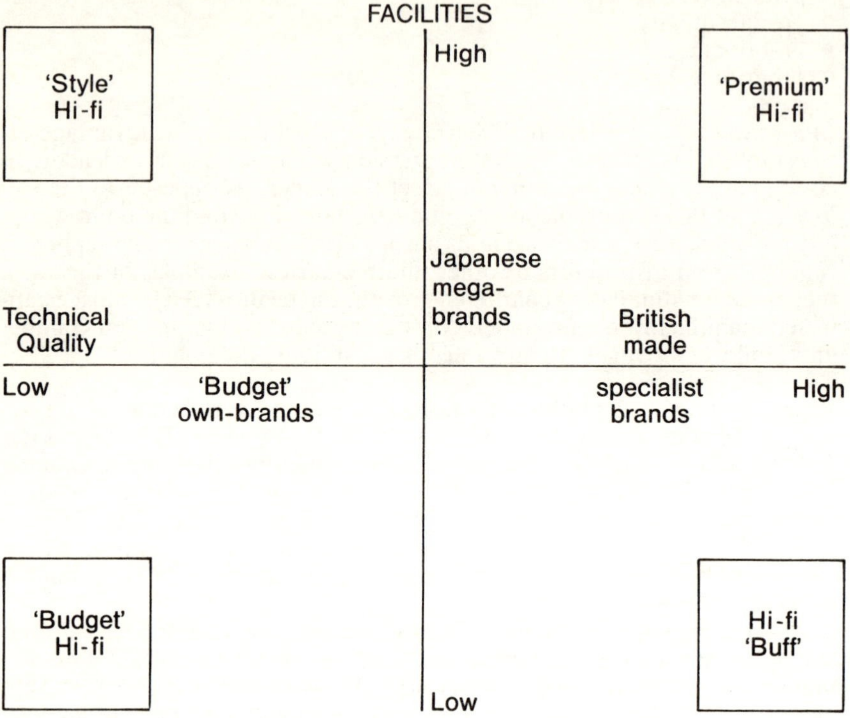

```
                              FACILITIES
┌──────────────┐              │ High              ┌──────────────┐
│              │              │                   │              │
│   'Style'    │              │                   │  'Premium'   │
│   Hi-fi      │              │                   │   Hi-fi      │
│              │              │                   │              │
└──────────────┘              │                   └──────────────┘

                              │ Japanese
                              │ mega-
  Technical                   │ brands      British
  Quality                     │             made
─────────────────────────────┼──────────────────────────────────
  Low         'Budget'        │             specialist      High
              own-brands      │             brands
                              │
                              │
┌──────────────┐              │                   ┌──────────────┐
│              │              │                   │              │
│   'Budget'   │              │                   │   Hi-fi      │
│   Hi-fi      │              │                   │   'Buff'     │
│              │              │                   │              │
└──────────────┘              │ Low               └──────────────┘
```

NOTES ON FIG 5.3

1. The axes should:
   - be based on factors that are critical to customer purchasing decisions, and
   - separate the offerings of different competitors.
2. The positioning of each competitor on the diagram will show the position of the nearest competitors and how best to counter them.
3. Different categories of customer may be identified by each segment of the chart.

Superior technology/manufacturing process   Superior technology is frequently the base of stronger competitors who may not be able to 'outsmart', but will be able to 'outspend'. A positioning based on technology may be useful in the early stages, but should be broadened before becoming a liability to the company. It is also an inherently limiting position: many customers are suspicious of technical leadership as, almost by definition, it is commercially unproven.

Marketing mix management

Marketing is an inherently simple discipline. It involves bringing customers and products together through the medium of:

1. pricing
2. advertising
3. direct sales effort
4. indirect sales effort
5. sales promotion.

These five factors are known as the *marketing mix*. The most important contribution marketing must make to a company's development is, as we have outlined above, the matching of a company's products to its customers' requirements. This involves market research, direct contact with customers and close interaction with the product development function. A marketing department cannot revitalise company performance through marketing mix management in the face of a product/customer mis-match.

Balancing the marketing mix can produce the optimum profit level for long-term continuance and development of the business. We consider each of the factors in turn below and then consider how these might be integrated into a successful marketing programme.

1. Pricing Pricing probably has the single most important impact on profitability. Most economists will argue that as price comes down the volume goes up. Whilst this may be true in general, the nature of this relationship can be affected by marketing action, eg advertising or sales promotion.

It is possible to achieve and sustain rapid growth through price cutting, but it is only commercially sound to do so where price is defended by scale or other cost advantages. Trading too heavily on a price platform can be dangerous when growth in the market slows or actually declines. The smaller company can often compete effectively on price as it avoids the 'overheads' of a large corporation. Growth inevitably destroys this advantage as the reasons for these 'overheads' become even more apparent to the growing company.

Low price also conveys low value and customers will respond to this. One should trade as far as possible on a value platform as outlined above. This is where understanding how a customer uses a product can make such an impact.

One should look to defend price by emphasising areas of competitive advantage. This in general ranks in the order:

- technical product superiority
- better performance in use
- better service
- greater consistency.

The company should choose the platform and deliver on it.

2. Advertising Advertising is an investment decision and should be treated as such. It should not be seen as a coming of age or a sign of respectability. It is appropriate for reaching a relatively wide number of consumers who cannot be accessed directly, or at least not economically. It is not appropriate when there are relatively few customers each of whom can be reached directly.

Advertising is part of the sales process and its role must be clearly defined. Different messages and media are appropriate according to the role the advertising is to play. This may be:

- encourage trial
- encourage increased usage levels
- defending existing consumption through reassurance.

As growth proceeds, the balance of advertising objectives will shift in this order. The work that the advertising is required to do should always be explicitly stated so that it can be adequately controlled.

Advertising copy also requires careful consideration. It must be consistent with the competitive advantage. If there is no relevant competitive advantage, advertising is unlikely to increase sales.

3. Direct sales effort   Personal selling effort is the hallmark of the newly established successful business. The personal sales conviction of the entrepreneur and his team is often critical to early success. In time, however, the needs of a growing business ensure that the founders spend less time on individual sales contacts. The inevitable result of this is that the business loses touch with its environment.

Whilst it is essential that senior management retains contact with customers they should not attempt close involvement with the day-to-day administration of selling. This requires sales professionals, not enthusiastic amateurs. There are, however, a number of pitfalls in moving to a professional sales force which need to be overcome.

Firstly, the tightly managed growing organisation will be reluctant to recruit in advance of a proven need and when it does eventually recruit, it may be reluctant to train salesmen adequately in product knowledge. There is no substitute for product knowledge, and a good salesman will insist upon this before committing himself to customers.

Once committed, however, the salesman must be held accountable for sales. Excessive interference from superiors will undermine his developing relationship with the company's customers.

No salesman should be recruited merely to serve the needs of existing customers. Each should be given time to prospect for new customers and to develop new relationships. This might seem wasteful in the growth cycle, but the wider range of contacts will prove more valuable in sustaining growth and resisting inroads from competitors.

It must not be forgotten that salesmen have eyes and ears, as well as a mouth. They are in touch with customers on a daily basis and listen to their views. They must be encouraged both to understand their customers and to articulate that understanding to the rest of the company.

Salesmen are notoriously poor communicators within their own companies and a special effort is required to see them as a two-way conduit for communication.

4. Indirect sales effort   Salesmen are a relatively costly means of taking orders. In addition to salary and commission there is inevitably a car and associated expenses. Salesmen's efforts should therefore be focused on that work which leads to the creation of an agreement to buy and to continue to do so. Effective salesmen are in short supply so it is necessary to subcontract as much of the routine activity as possible to other parts of the organisation.

Frequently, this may involve the use of a 'Telesales' operation. It is important to understand the widely differing roles that a telesales operation may play:

- booking appointments for established contacts
- cold-calling on potential new contacts
- responding to customer calls, perhaps stimulated by a mailshot or advertisement
- technical support
- chasing call-off orders against an agreed sale
- co-ordinating sales drops to maximise distribution efficiency.

Some or all of these activities may be subcontracted to specialist agencies. Whether this is feasible or desirable will depend very much on the dynamics of the industry that the company serves, and the requirements of its customers.

It is pointless to try to sell aggressively to customers who are not in a position to buy—it only irritates them. The telesales operation should not normally be used to finalise a contract—that is the role of the salesman—the role of telesales is to create the environment where the salesman has the optimum chance of completing the deal.

5. Sales promotion There are many ways that sales can be enhanced, other than through advertising, and we group these under the heading of Sales Promotion. They encompass:

- dealer incentive programmes
- consumer incentives
- direct mail.

The form and substance of these approaches rest heavily on creativity. Some fascinating and exciting approaches can be derived; many, however, will have more interest value than positive financial impact.

While the objective of any sales promotion programme is to create interest, that interest must be firmly tied to the underlying benefits of the products or services that are being sold. That is, they should be wholly consistent with, and support, the positioning of the product, as outlined above.

If the company sells through distributors or intermediaries, it will need their goodwill to promote its products. The extent to which this can be achieved varies according to the industry, in some they are totally banned. At their worst, these schemes are only marginally legal and of dubious ethics. Management should avoid schemes that merely pass money to dealers/employees.

Schemes that provide training for dealer's staff or which can be related to their performance in their job are much more likely to be acceptable to all partners and in the long run more effective.

Most current consumer incentive programmes are either straight 'money-off' next purchase or 'free extra product' promotions. As such, they are disguised price cutting and should be used as a short-term tactical means of cutting price to reduce stock levels without inciting an aggressive response from competitors. If used too frequently these schemes can have the same impact as price cutting in terms of long-term degradation of product image.

Other forms of incentive involve either a free 'product' after so many purchases or the offer to buy a product at lower price. In both cases the product on offer should be clearly associated with the product you are trying to sell and, if at all possible, boost its consumption. For example, the branded chocolate drinking mug offered by Cadbury's.

As a company grows, it becomes more and more dependent upon repeat purchases. Some form of loyalty bonus may therefore be attractive in sustaining growth.

This may be of the 'Green Shield Stamp' variety as recently being used to promote credit card use; or they may be much more informal. For example, relatively high trade-in values on the earlier models sold might be presented as loyalty bonuses (whereas in fact they are discounts).

Conclusion

As a company grows there is a tendency to add departments or support functions as appendages to the business rather than components of it. As a result, growth leads to a loss of cohesion.

The underlying reason for growth is a satisfied customer. If the company is to continue to grow that must become the focus of the organisation. Marketing's real role is to focus and co-ordinate the company's effort on maintaining customer satisfaction.

Marketing cannot operate effectively in a growing company where it is treated as a department for organising exhibitions and attending trade functions. If marketing is to work, it is likely to be an uncomfortable experience; it will involve change throughout the company:

- in R & D which will have to share responsibility for new products and take its leadership from marketing
- in sales who will have to sacrifice the comfortable in pursuit of the profitable
- in manufacturing and logistics who will have new standards of 'on-specification' and 'on-time' to adhere to (more space is given to this subject in the next chapter)
- in accounts who will have to provide management information rather than transactions data.

Internal communication will have to be frequent and positive if marketing is to have the necessary impact on a growing company.

Marketing provides the interface between the customer and the company. It is an essential discipline if the growing company is to continue to prosper, but it is one that can only work if it touches the heart of the company.

CHAPTER 6

Operations Management

Introduction

'Production and distribution are simply the means of meeting customers' needs. Please discuss.'

This could be a question in the final paper of an Operations Management degree course. The examiner, on receiving the reply 'agreed', whilst feeling that the examinee had come down on the right side of the fence, might feel aggrieved that a fuller explanation had not been attempted. This chapter provides a slightly extended explanation of our examinee's agreement.

Those production managers who feel that their only role is to maximise resource utilisation, or those distribution managers whose sole ambition is to deliver from factory to customer at least cost may find this chapter challenging. The operations manager must be outward looking. He must look toward the strategic plans for the business, toward the strategies for marketing and new product development and toward the business' customers and suppliers.

This is especially true for the operations manager in a growing company. The business' aspirations should be translated into a detailed plan which should take into account the resource capacity, machinery, personnel and the finance required to fund investment in plant and training.

A key to the success of a growing company is the relationship it maintains with customers and suppliers: knowing precisely what the customer needs and then providing it, whilst identifying precisely its own requirements from suppliers and assisting them in providing it. Management must be committed to quality as a means of meeting customers' needs and this can only be achieved after a sound relationship has been established with suppliers.

Growth frequently produces product complexity; complexity in terms of extending technological capability, complexity in terms of scheduling more products and complexity in terms of the diverse handling characteristics of an extended product range in distribution.

Clearly, in having been successful to date in achieving growth, the company must have already, to some extent, come to terms with these issues. However, through development, changes will occur: growth in staff creates a need for changes in management style and previously informal channels of internal and external communication become fragmented, as companies become more functionalised. At this time the company must adopt a more formal and structured approach to managing its operations.

'Operations' has four key roles in a growing company, as shown in Fig 6.1 on page 106; these are:

Fig 6.1: Operation's Role

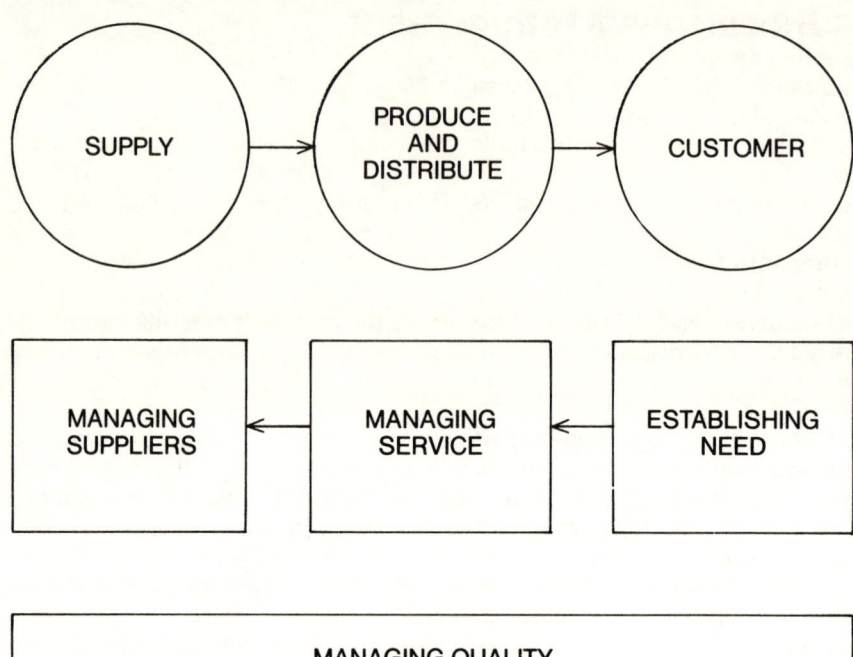

- establishing customer needs
- managing customer service
- managing suppliers
- managing quality.

Establishing customer needs

Any discussion on operations management must start with the customer. The first step is to examine how operations might respond to each category of customer need, as identified below. In order to do this the growing company must establish what its customers' needs are. These issues are discussed in greater detail below.

Categories of customer need

Customers typically express their needs within the parameters of:

- product range
- product quality
- the service package.

Product range   Companies increasingly appreciate the benefit of, and are implementing strategies to achieve, a reduction in their supplier base; the benefit of this for the growing company is discussed further in this chapter under the section 'Managing Suppliers'. This implies that companies would wish to source a greater range of products from a narrow supplier base: the engine assembler will wish to acquire all his castings from one foundry; the car manufacturer will want to buy the full range of metal fastenings from one machining shop; the food processor will want to buy all his flavourings from one ingredient manufacturer.

Therefore, to make itself a more attractive supplier, the implication is that the growing company must consider a strategy of manufacturing a more comprehensive range of products. This strategy can be challenged on two fronts:

Firstly, extension of the range may dilute the company's competitive advantage by re-directing the business from products where it has a technical advantage, towards those where it has not; and extension of the range may remove cost advantages gained from product-specific machinery, since more flexible machinery may be required.

Secondly, offering a greater range to customers need not necessarily mean manufacturing it. Sub-contracting specialist products to third parties that possess the appropriate technology is often a more effective solution. A company manufacturing softwood doors may secure major building merchant accounts by offering some hardwood doors in its range accounting for, say, just 2% of sales. However, it may not be economic to invest in plant capable of machining hardwood and so the company should sub-contract this manufacture to hardwood specialists.

On the other hand, operation's role is also to contribute in identifying where the existing technology can meet market opportunity. For example, the same door manufacturer may have an opportunity to provide a complete package of softwood doors and softwood frames to builders merchants: ie same raw materials, same technology, same handling characteristics. The product range has thus been extended, perhaps without an increase in fixed costs, and this is accordingly a more attractive proposition.

Product quality It is not difficult to persuade customers to talk about their needs for product quality; but it is more difficult to interpret exactly what it is that they require. They may use adjectives such as 'top', 'high', 'excellent', 'best', when asked to describe their quality requirements. However, the food manufacturer does not need packaging which will protect his product in sub-arctic temperatures for ten years—particularly if the product's shelf-life is three weeks and it is kept in a temperature controlled environment. In this case the customer needs packaging material which runs efficiently through his machines with minimum waste, protects his product during transportation and looks attractive when displayed on the supermarket shelf.

Products must meet customers' needs, but not exceed them if by doing so cost has been added to the product. Others have coined the phase 'conforming to requirements' and like the food manufacturer, requirements can be classified into *performance* needs and *appearance* needs.

The first step is to request the customer to define the performance needs and appearance needs of the product and to develop with him a product specification. The combination of complete knowledge of customers' needs, and the technical input of the supplier in his specialist manufacturing area, may allow the supplier to create a higher quality product solution than his customer would have otherwise independently specified. It could be 'higher quality' because it conforms to the customer's requirements more precisely and at lower cost.

The service package   The customer service package has components of:

- delivering the product
- service after delivery, and
- ongoing support.

In *delivering the product* it is important to isolate the key factors perceived as important by the customer. Is it the lead time that occurs between order placement and delivery, is it the frequency of delivery, or is it simply reliability, ie arriving at the customer when promised and with product that matches the order exactly?

Although, of these, delivery frequency has obvious transport cost implications, lead time is usually the issue which has the most dramatic implications for the manufacturer. If the company cannot provide raw materials, manufacture and deliver within these lead times, then inventory must be stored elsewhere in the supply chain. Inventory immediately adds to costs—stores or warehouse space, storage and handling equipment cost—and requires skills—inventory reordering, demand forecasting and stores management.

These inventory costs and skills requirements may be avoided by more careful consideration and discussion with the customer to identify opportunities to reduce and refine lead times.

The requirements for *service after delivery* and *ongoing support* are very much more industry specific. International Computers Limited (ICL) gives detailed attention to service for their computers after installation. Therefore, their service logistics are more complex than the logistics for delivery and installation, whilst Mars Confectionery customers have little need for service after delivery. On the other hand Mars provides a high level of support to its retailing customers to provide advice on display of confectionery to maximise sales of their product.

So far in this section categories of customer need have been identified. The discussion which follows will consider how the growing company establishes its customers' needs.

Finding out customer needs

As the company grows, relationships with customers will change. These, often previously conducted on a day-to-day basis by directors of the company, are now delegated as the number of customers expands. Consequently, at this stage, policies for service must be more formally stated and implemented and their success measured, reviewed and adjusted accordingly.

However, how can a company establish the needs of its customers? The most obvious means is to ask them, since, by doing so the company will demonstrate its interest in meeting their needs. Unfortunately, customer contacts are usually in 'selling mode' or in 'complaint mode'. The former is unlikely to provide accurate data on the cutomer's real needs, since both salesman and buyer adopt negotiating stances. The latter, complaint mode, is dealing with a distressed situation where, with a dissatisfied customer, the scope for constructive comment on the overall balance of his needs is, at best, likely to be blinkered by the specific situation. This is not to say that internal diagnosis of customer complaints, to identify corrective action, has no place in operations management.

Customer needs can only be established accurately if the information collection exercise is carried out over and above normal day-to-day business discussions and, in some situations, by third party agencies. There is a need for a customer survey which should take the form of an interview where customers are requested to rank their needs, comment on how well the company meets these needs, and how well it performs against the competition in meeting them. The outputs of this exercise, if conducted against a properly representative sample of customers, will prescribe the actions that must be taken to compete more effectively.

Having established customers' needs, there are four factors that should be established to reap rewards from the analysis:

- determine the service policies which will meet customers' needs
- develop a strategy to deliver them
- monitor the performance against it internally, and
- check for customer satisfaction to ensure that the company's service policies meet their needs.

If the company is able to deliver a level of service performance that the competition cannot, in areas that are important to customers, then the business has a strong competitive edge which can often command premium prices. A customer survey carried out in 1989 for a building products manufacturer revealed customer service to be more important than product quality, with price the least important factor. Consistent performance on reliable delivery, measured by order fill and delivery timeliness would command, in this instance, a 5% price premium.

The remainder of this chapter examines operations' role in meeting customer needs.

Managing customer service

The service policies have been determined: the operations manager's job is to deliver. The first task, as emphasised throughout this book, is to develop a strategy.

Strategy

The company must establish the components of its operations strategy to enable it to deliver its service mission. There are two interlinked components to an operations strategy as shown in Fig 6.2 (page 110), these are production and distribution. Together they form the logistics strategy.

The production strategy needs only resolve the issue of the order penetration point (OPP): being the point in the manufacturing process at which product becomes allocated to a specific customer. The Ford Motor

Fig 6.2: Operations Strategy

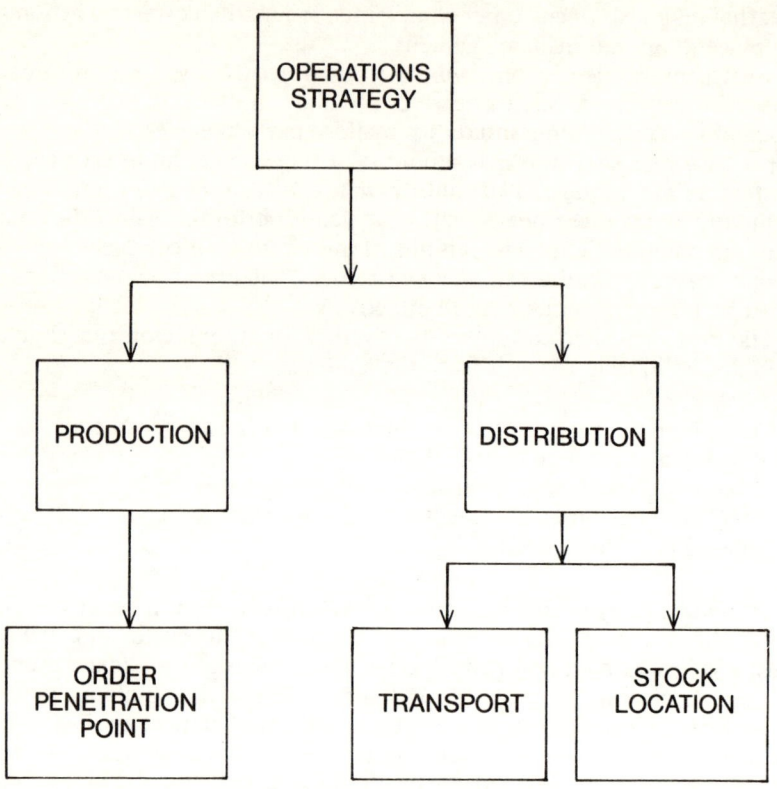

Company in the UK has its OPP in the finished car compound—the dealers'
name and address is attached to the car. Rolls Royce cars are allocated
to customers prior to the car body being painted.

The distribution strategy needs to answer two questions at most: where
should stocks of finished product be held, and how should product be
transported to the customer? If the OPP is in the manufacturing process,
then only the transport issues need to be addressed, as there will be no
warehouse in the distribution cycle and hence no stockholding issues. If the
OPP is in distribution, the food industry being a prime example where
product is allocated to supermarkets from regional depots, then the distribution strategy should aim to deliver within the lead time required by the
customer at a minimum combined cost in warehousing and transport.

Complex depot location models are available and used extensively within
fast moving consumer goods industries. However, often a pertinent question to be asked is, 'do I need depots at all?', since a depot immediately
results in incremental overheads. One UK metal fastenings manufacturer,
for example, air freights rivets to customers in Japan to avoid the high costs
of warehousing in that country.

There is a role for the operations manager within the logistics strategy
formulation process, to add value to the overall business.

Added value logistics

Whilst opportunities are specific to individual companies, industries and markets, there are common areas where logistics concepts can add value to the business.

Moving the order penetration point A critical factor is that the OPP should come as early as possible in the supply chain, since this will reward the company with significant improvements in its performance, as illustrated in Fig 6.3 below. A company constructing a paper mill in Northern Europe planned to have the OPP at its finished goods warehouse thereby meeting its European customers' orders within seven days from a wide range of cut sheet and reel specification stocks. By introducing improved methods for sales order processing and production scheduling they can now plan to allocate paper to customers from the output of the paper making machine. The mill is now being constructed on the assumption of holding 50% less stock, and storage space, and the financial projections for the operation assume less capital costs for warehousing and reduced operations costs for paper waste in the finishing operations.

Reducing total lead time In simple terms, a lead time comprises order administration, production and delivery. A false assumption is often made that these activities must occur in series, one after the other, whereas in many situations total lead time can be reduced by overlapping them as shown in Fig 6.4 (page 112).

Fig 6.3: Order Penetration Point

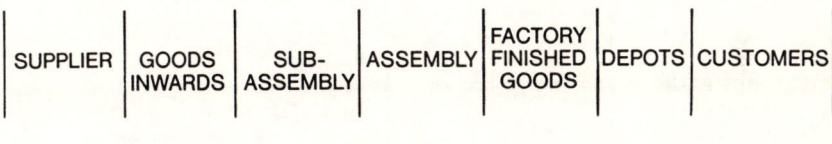

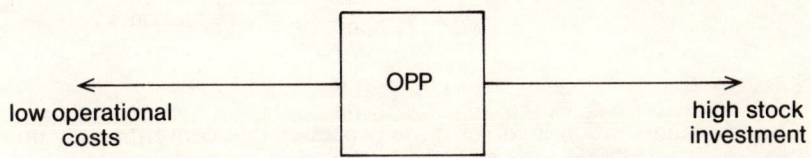

Fig 6.4: Lead Time

BEFORE

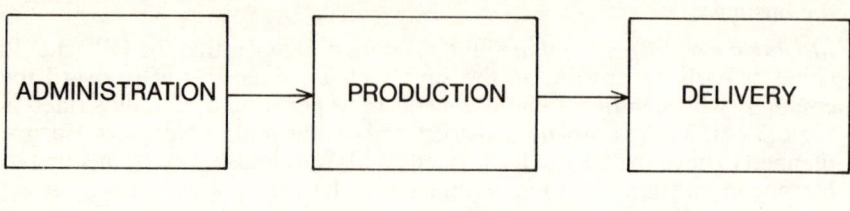

AFTER

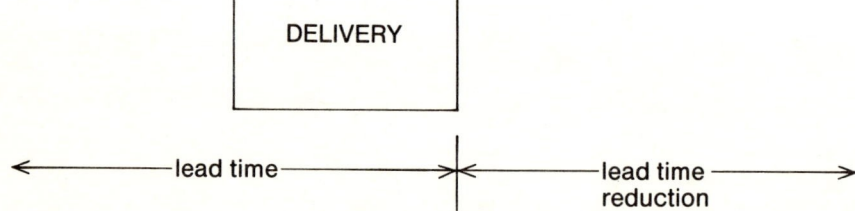

Order administration involves those processes that conventionally must occur between the customer establishing his need for the company's products, through product specification, through order documentation creation, through order transmission, order receipt and the conversion of the order into a document that operations can work to—the works order. In some industries this may involve weeks, in others months. However, much of this can be eliminated through the use of the telephone or facsimile machine. 'You will be receiving order confirmation for x of your products. Please commence production immediately.' The time it takes to process the order is not then part of an overall lead time. DIY retailers pursue this policy with their suppliers and they have even dispensed with order confirmation as a process.

Does the customer require delivery of the complete order on his stated delivery date? A printer who is setting up his presses for a print run (which can take several hours) only needs one reel of paper at set-up. The other reels are required later, at commencement of the print run. The few extra hours of lead time thus generated may allow the paper supplier to finish paper to order, and overlap production with delivery to reduce the total lead time.

Logistics friendly design   There are two common areas where design can reduce cost in logistics. The first is by maximising commonality of components within and across product lines. This reduces investment in component stocks and storage space and reduces the likelihood of stock-outs. For many years, a yoghurt producer in the UK accepted his marketing colleague's requirement for a different container for own label product from branded product, thereby doubling the range of finished goods. The requirement disappeared when a multi-million pound investment was required to warehouse them.

The second is by reducing the number of components in a product. Warehouse racking manufacturers have moved away from designs specifically engineered for customers' warehouses, to flexible construction kits consisting of three standard components—the upright, the beam, and the cross-ties. Order lead times and manufacturer's stocks are considerably reduced.

Managing sales agents   In a number of industries, a company's success depends upon the effectiveness of third party sales agents. The motor industry is a prime example, where the success of dealers, both in initial sales and after sales care, is essential to the success of the car manufacturer. Many manufacurers, in recognising this, undertake on-going dealership management programmes—both in the strategic and operations aspects of its dealers' business. This is not necessarily straightforward since the manufacturer can only either consult with, or offer business incentives to, but never take management decisions for, third party businesses. BMW (GB), for example, does not accept an arm's-length relationship with its dealers; it trains its dealers in parts stock management, and allocates a BMW manager to work with each dealer's parts manager to achieve business goals, for example immediate off-shelf ('first pick') parts availability, which are compatible with BMW's own goals for after sales service.

Logistics by market sector   It is important that the customer service mission is market specific, rather than a compromise which nearly satisfies everyone, actually satisfies no-one, but exists because the business considers that it cannot cope with differentiating its approach between customers. Brewing is a good example where customers fall into two camps; the tenanted or managed public house, and the independent off-licence trade. The public house needs reliability; regular timetabled deliveries so that staff are available to receive stock. The independent trade needs short order lead times because demand for the product is highly volatile, driven by climate, promotions and the 'party' seasons. The logistics approach must be differentiated to recognise these differences; regular runs using scheduled but infrequent deliveries with large articulated lorries to minimise distribution costs to public houses; smaller next-day delivery vans which can be called from local depots at short notice to the independent. Although more costly to the independent trade this latter method satisfies their main requirement which is to minimise lead times.

Priority allocation rules   In some companies, the differentiation is not by market, but by urgency of need. Health care is a prime example. A particular product may be sold either to pharmacists, but also needs to meet a 100% satisfaction level within 12 hours at hospitals. Clearly, the manufacturer will maintain one stock of the product to meet both groups of customers at the stated levels of satisfaction, since separate stockholdings will inflate overall stock requirements. However, priority allocation rules must be observed at times of stock shortages. This may take the form of a 'reserved' stock level for hospital demands, or reallocating product away from pharmacists' orders, or even systems which buy back product from pharmacists to meet hospital shortfalls.

Measures of service performance

As was stated earlier, a key element in managing the delivery of service is to establish measures of performance and to monitor the business against these measures.

It is impossible to chronicle all measures of operations performance to suit every potential business situation; impossible and counter-productive. Performance measures should be few, relevant, and reviewed regularly.

Management teams will find it difficult to absorb more than half a dozen business performance indicators. Since 'profit' and 'cash' account for two of these, then the operational performance of the business must be captured in no more than three or four key measures.

Business performance measures must closely correspond to customers' specific needs: if the customer requires a short lead time, measure lead time average, worst and best; if the customer requires reliable supply, measure percentage customer satisfaction; if the customer requires a fixed delivery schedule, measure the number of on-time, late and early deliveries. In each of these examples, labour efficiency, resource utilisation and other more traditional measures of operations performance are irrelevant and should not feature in management reviews, since if they do so they will be a distraction from critical measures.

As the company grows, so it requires the support of a more formalised organisation structure. It is of fundamental importance that each element of the company has objectives and performance measures in areas that directly effect the overall strategy of the business—that is, meeting customers' needs. Take for example an organisation which separates logistics and production into two departments in a business which strives for high customer satisfaction. The production schedule shows capacity to produce five batches of product, but the logistics department, to maintain stock levels, calls for half-batches of ten different products. The production manager, tasked to minimise costs through high resource utilisation is in a difficult position, since product changes lower utilisation and increase costs. This dilemma is avoided by abandoning utilisation and cost targets and by introducing order schedule adherence as the production objective.

Performance measures must be at least informative, but at best prescriptive of corrective actions that are required to be taken by management. A report that shows a 50% success rate at meeting pre-arranged delivery times to a customer is informative. A report that shows the previous customer on this particular route keeps the driver waiting an average two hours is prescriptive. Ideally, sufficient backup information needs to be available to prescribe corrective action. However, regular collection of such prescriptive data may burden the company with too onerous a data collection exercise, and specific analyses may be required to prescribe the problem.

Performance measures which are misleading must be avoided. Builders require, above all, reliable delivery from their suppliers, since materials must be available when labour is hired, but builders do not require short lead times. A building products manufacturer recognising this, adjusts the builder's order in the light of product availability and sends advance acknowledgement of when the products will be despatched. In this example, reliability performance is monitored by recording actual delivery against acknowledgement, and achievement is 98%. A relevant measure of performance and a strong result you may think. The same manufacturer also supplies builders merchants, where stock service on very short lead times is crucial since business is built on ability to stock or supply quickly. The manufacturer used the same measure of performance, percentage of order acknowledgements delivered, to monitor success in builders merchants until it was pointed out that 25% of merchants' orders were not being met because of stock shortages prior to delivery. Merchants were receiving 75% stock service, the business was reporting 98%. The performance measure used was misleading and was causing a loss of business to the competition.

Clearly, the role of the operations manager is vital in managing service successfully. It requires strategic and innovative ability: strategic ability to define the operations infrastructure that is required to deliver customer needs, and innovative ability to identify opportunities in operations so as to gain a competitive edge.

Next, consideration is given to the contribution that suppliers make to the growing company.

Managing suppliers

Supplier performance presents a major variant to the success of any business in reaching its goal of satisfying customer needs; this is particularly so in the growing company. The operations manager may feel that he cannot afford to devote manpower to managing suppliers: this section will assert that he cannot afford not to. Typically, in a manufacturing company, purchased materials represent 50% of the cost of the finished product. As a measure, a growing company may need to allocate at least 50% of its operations manpower to *developing* the performance it needs from its suppliers, possibly reducing to no less than 25% to *maintain* performance at required levels.

The major difficulty faced by growing companies is where to start.

Priorities for managing suppliers

The purchasing department must establish priorities upon which to focus the management of supply. This can be done by assessing the impact of poor supply performance on the business. To do this the following component ranking criteria have been found to be useful:

- *sales value*   Ranking supplied components by the total contribution that they make to the business' sales value
- *commonality*   Poor supply performance for a component which is widely used across a range of finished products will have a serious impact on the company's ability to service its customers, and
- *bottleneck components*   Bought-in items which consume scarce resources must have good supply: poor quality materials or late delivery will directly affect the total output from the plant.

The next step in establishing priorities is to rank components by actual supply performance on the criteria of *quality* and *delivery*.

Priorities for improving suppliers' performance can then be given to those products that have both a high impact on the business and have a poor supply performance. Experience shows that this component analysis will separate the poor suppliers from the good suppliers, so that the purchasing department can focus its attention on poor suppliers. Illustratively, this means placing priority on managing improvements in suppliers who dominate the top right hand corner of the matrix in Fig 6.5 below, before moving onto other suppliers.

Fig 6.5: Priorities for Supplier Management

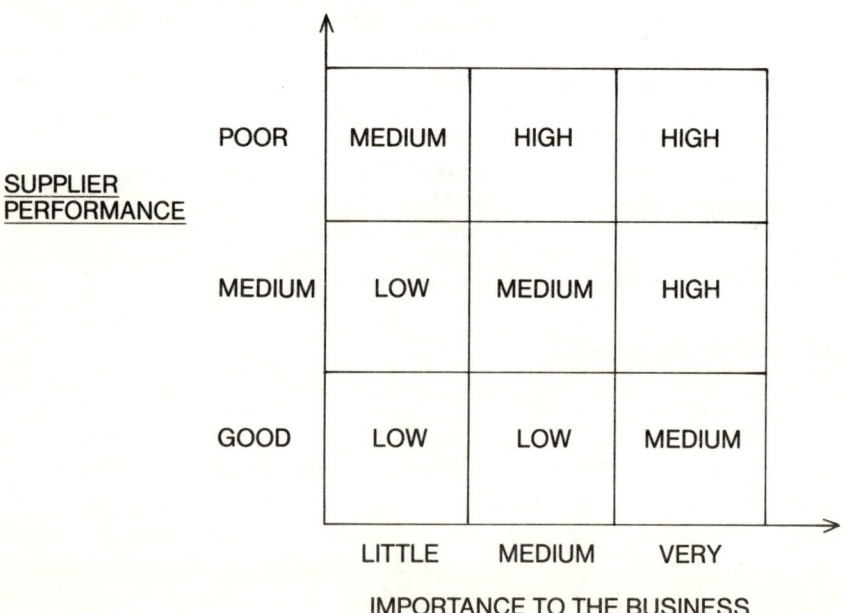

There are a number of constructive means by which the business can assist its suppliers to improve the quality and delivery of their products.

Improving supplier quality

Most companies concentrate on specifying the *design* of the components they need from their suppliers; material specifications and tolerances and occasionally the production methods to be used. However, what they really require is that the component meets *performance* criteria. By specifying design, the company is bypassing the possibility that its suppliers may be able to innovate to generate a higher quality design: higher quality in that it meets the performance requirements at lower cost. Some companies, such as Kawasaki in the USA, take the view that since they have elected to buy-out components rather than make-in, then the supplier has greater expertise in their design and manufacture than they have. Consequently, they specify performance rather than design.

Supplier quality improvements will be made through closer working relationships. Inviting suppliers to the company to observe how their components are used stimulates ideas for improvements in quality. Visiting suppliers' premises to assist in improving their process of quality control produces benefits to both parties. The earlier that quality problems are highlighted, the less costly they are to the supplier, and the resultant improvements in component quality will benefit both supplier and customer.

Improving supplier delivery

The most common cause of poor supplier delivery performance is the instability of the orders that the business gives to its suppliers. The more an order is amended, the more difficult it is to respond. Ability to communicate updated orders efficiently has been improved through the use of information technology, for example electronic data interchange (EDI). However, this does not necessarily ensure that the supplier is able to respond.

There are means by which these difficulties can be minimised by working more closely with suppliers. The first is to establish a *frozen zone*, making the earliest part of an order schedule firm, adjusting only subsequent parts of the schedule, thus giving the supplier time to react. Secondly, *families of products* can be sourced from one supplier: increases in requirements of some components in the family may be balanced by a reduction in others, enabling the supplier to improve response. Thirdly, *early commitment* to capacity and/or raw materials may enable the suppliers to react to exact manufacturing quantities specified much nearer to the due date. Finally, it is essential to issue schedules synchronised with suppliers' planning systems. For example, if the supplier runs his materials requirement planning system each Monday, receiving vendor schedules on Tuesday adds one week to the lead time.

Clearly, for a company purchasing a wide range of components from a diverse supplier base, the task of managing suppliers is onerous. The benefits of rationalising the number of components used has already been discussed in this chapter; simplifying the supplier base also has important benefits in focusing supplier management on a reduced number of targets. Many companies, in the automotive industry for example, are moving toward single sourcing as they realise that dual sourcing does not address the causes of poor supplier performance; it simply makes one supplier's performance look acceptable in the light of a poor performance from the other.

The performance measures that are set for a purchasing department are the keys to unlock improved supplier performance, since they encapsulate the department's objectives.

Measuring the performance of a purchasing department

A purchasing department should be measured on its performance in developing its supplier base, and on the performance of its suppliers. Below we give some simple examples under these two areas.

Supplier base development   The purchasing department's performance can be assessed from the skill with which the supplier base is managed. This can be monitored by reductions in the base from one period to the next. The proportion of suppliers achieving performance standards, and the value of cost reduction projects initiated at suppliers, are effective means of assessing how well the purchasing department is managing and motivating its suppliers.

Suppliers' performance   Suppliers should be measured *absolutely* and *relatively*: absolutely on their current performance against the company's needs, and relatively on the improvement in the current period against the previous period. The measures used relate to supply *quality* and supply *delivery*: the total cost of quality to the business for parts received from the supplier, and the number of components received from the supplier on time compared with schedule. The total cost of quality is discussed later in this chapter, but briefly includes all costs associated with securing conformity to requirements: the cost of resource in developing suppliers, the cost of quality checking on receipt, the cost of scrap or reworking faulty components, the cost of machine downtime due to faulty components and the component purchase price.

Finally, it is important to note the emphasis placed here on measuring the purchasing department in terms of the quality and delivery performance enjoyed by the business. However, there is still room to measure economic performance alongside these other measures: material purchase prices, the size and overheads of the purchasing department are values which can be compared with industry standards or with performance in previous periods.

We have discussed the role of supplier management in meeting the needs of customers of the growing company. In doing so we highlighted supplier quality as a key issue. We now look at how in-house quality must be managed.

Managing quality

Earlier in this chapter we discussed how the company might establish its customers' product quality needs and we used the term 'conforming to requirement'. The company should be managed to manufacture products which conform to customers' requirements by focusing on the culture and attitude needed to achieve *total quality management* (TQM). This is an approach now widely adopted by mature companies as an ongoing process for reducing manufacturing cost. It is reported that ITT in the USA reduced its cost of quality from 18% to 5% of sales value between 1967–1977, the difference being reflected in bottom line profitability. These prolonged timescales may be due to the difficulty of changing entrenched attitudes within mature organisations. In a growing company, the size of potential benefits from TQM are just as large, but it may be possible to achieve them more rapidly if the culture and attitude is correct from the outset.

Once the definition of quality as 'conformance to requirement' is fully understood by the organisation, there are then three interlinked components, shown in Fig 6.6 below, to TQM: *management participation, the role of the quality manager,* and the *total cost of quality measurement*.

100% commitment from all managers is necessary to achieve a suitable culture and attitude. Arm's-length support, caveated approval or lip-service to the TQM programme are not just insufficient but are counter-productive. Senior management has to be active in their belief of TQM. A single-minded devotion to the achievement of quality in the delivery of customers' needs must be a key part of strategy. The effect upon the culture of the business of just one example of management 'turning a blind eye' or advocating the

Fig 6.6: Total Quality Management

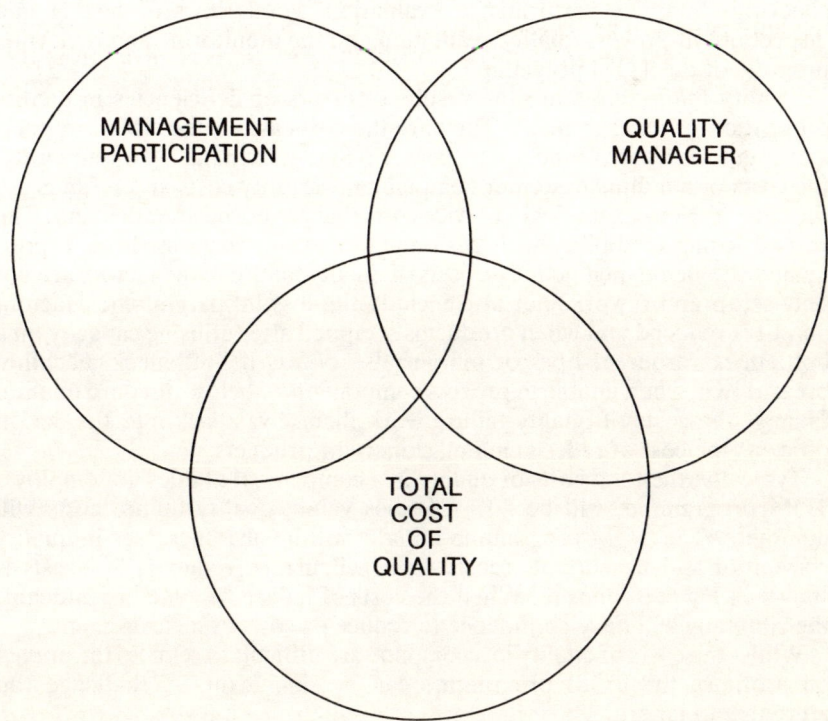

despatch of quality not conforming to requirement may take years to reverse.

The role of the quality manager is to improve the company's attitude to quality and to initiate projects to improve quality. He is responsible for the quality improvement programme. However, the quality manager is *not* the custodian of the company's quality performance—the operational managers are and the quality manager merely assists them. Quality projects are *not* carried out by the quality manager, but by the operational managers. The quality department is thus not a vast empire of people; typically the growing company will require one person, but to reflect the importance of TQM to the business, the quality manager will have a seat at management meetings. Therefore, the quality manager needs to be a quality professional and it is likely that a growing company will need to recruit an individual with the appropriate experience from outside the organisation.

The company's goal is to reduce the total cost of quality. Therefore, the elements of the total cost of quality must be defined, regularly measured and reviewed at management meetings. The company should include in its costs everything associated with *preventing* quality problems, *measuring* quality performance and quality *failure*.

Quality *prevention* costs start with the supplier, as we discussed earlier; they are the resources of the purchasing department devoted to working with suppliers to improve their performance. The time spent in activities associated with the TQM programme itself are included; quality training, orientation and project work. Much of the work in engineering design is the cost of quality; design reviews, drawing checking, innovation. Finally, preventative maintenance and tool control are quality prevention costs.

Quality *measurement* costs include all aspects of quality auditing and checking. Supplier performance evaluation, goods inwards testing and inspection, in-process quality evaluation and the monitoring and reviewing progress of the TQM progamme.

Quality *failure* costs are the results of errors or deficiencies in quality prevention or measurement. They are the costs associated when products and components are found not to 'conform to requirements'. Consequently, the costs of handling customer complaints, warranty costs and refunds are the most obvious examples of service costs that are borne after delivery. The cost of losing credibility with customers or losing business through poor quality should be included. The costs of quality failure in the factory are not only scrap and rework, but also include the loss in margin when factory output is reduced and when product is scrapped after utilising capacity on a bottleneck resource. Loss of margin also occurs if bottleneck machines break down, when unable to process components of below standard quality. Finally, the costs of quality failure work themselves back into the design office as the cost of redesigning machinery or products.

Typically, the total costs of quality in a company, that does not employ a TQM programme, will be 20% of sales value; quality failure costs will dominate. The TQM programme initially will involve increases in quality prevention and measurement costs which will, in turn, reduce failure costs as shown in Fig 6.7 opposite. When the costs of failure become insignificant, the company will have confidence to reduce its costs of measurement.

Whilst the costs of quality in a company are difficult to reduce, the impact on profit of the TQM programme can be significant. A challenge too attractive to ignore.

Fig 6.7: Total Cost of Quality

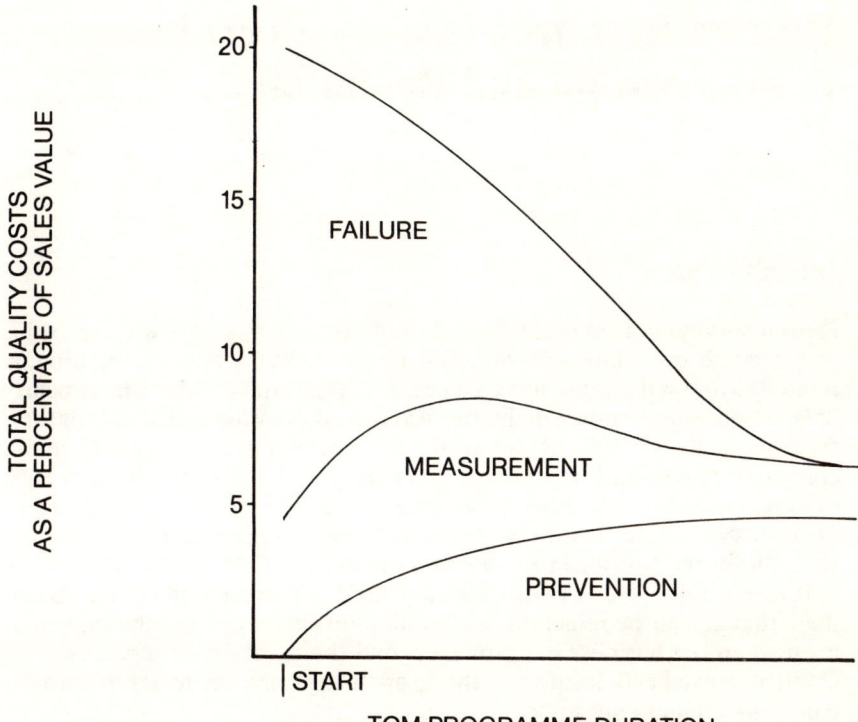

Conclusion

This chapter has outlined the key tasks of the operations manager in a growing company; a single-minded devotion to delivery of the service required by customers which is underpinned by total quality management. The importance of supplier performance in service delivery has also been stressed.

The twin goals of customer satisfaction and total quality management create a synergy: both require the complete commitment of the operations manager, as priorities above all other issues, such as resource utilisation objectives. 'We may get away with it' is not an attitude which will ensure growth; but it will demotivate a workforce. People want to work in companies which meet their customers' needs by striving for quality. Companies that address these issues successfully gain a major competitive advantage in attracting and retaining the best employees, since care for the customer is complimentary to care for the employee and thus assists in creating constructive relationships between employee and employer. Human resource issues are now discussed in greater detail.

CHAPTER 7

Human Resource Issues—Recruitment, Remuneration and Retention

Introduction

Recent surveys indicate that current shortages of employees with key skills will become even more pronounced in the 1990s; a fact that is directly related to major demographic changes. The Western World will have nearly 25% less men and women in the 16–24 age bracket by the end of the century. By 1995 just over 70% of the available workforce will be aged 25 to 54, compared to 65% in 1987 and it is also anticipated that approximately 80% of new positions will be filled by women. Within Western Europe, a further factor to be considered is the potential for free movement of labour particularly within the European Economic Community.

It is often the case, where a business has been developed by one individual, that he may be reluctant to relax his hold over aspects of the company, even when the business has grown beyond the capabilities of one person. Control must be delegated if the growth experienced to date is to be consolidated and built upon.

Against this background, growing companies must give careful consideration not only to recruitment but should also ensure that they reward and retain key staff at all levels. Retention and remuneration programmes will assume even greater importance in the 1990s and beyond.

In this chapter we examine the most important human resource issues that confront growing companies, placing particular emphasis upon practical guidelines for recruitment and retention.

Manpower planning

The development of a realistic and relevant manpower plan is essential before any action is taken to create a new position or to make an appointment—whether this be from within the organisation or through external recruitment. The manpower plan should be closely related to the overall corporate strategy and it should form an integral part of the business plan. This plan should take account of the current and proposed organisation structure at company and departmental level.

Central to the manpower plan is a detailed and up to date review of the current available workforce. This should take account of factors such as headcount budgets, the impact of the introduction of new manufacturing techniques, the effect of increased sales promotions, the introduction of new information technology, anticipated leavers, etc. The available skills at all levels within the organisation should be closely allied to future requirements so as to initiate either training or education action plans, internal transfers/ promotions or external recruitment. Age distribution throughout the organisation should also be considered as an important factor.

Responsibility for the development of the manpower plan should rest with senior management who should also ensure that it meets the current and future requirements of the organisation. Any dedicated personnel manager or personnel function should be charged with assisting in the implementation of the plan, which is the responsibility of the senior management team rather than being an isolated personnel activity. The manpower plan need not be a rigorously defined or complicated document but should be sufficiently flexible to cope with the changing needs of the company and must interlock with the proposed structure and strategy of the business.

Recruitment

Job definition

Following development of the manpower plan, which will identify any requirements for extra staff or an increased level of skills, there are several steps which should be considered as important prerequisites prior to any internal or external action is taken to fill a vacancy. These are easily dealt with and do not require any specific training or skill, but they are critically important if the manpower plan is to be followed and people are to be employed effectively.

The position under consideration should be subject to an overview, avoiding detailed analysis but concentrating on the key aspects of the job. The following areas should be briefly considered: what the position involves, how it interfaces with other jobs, the level of experience, skill and knowledge required, the type of individual that the job requires, the contribution that it makes to the organisation and any particular difficulties which the employee is likely to encounter. At this stage it is not always appropriate to refer to the existing job description, for there may have been many small, but important changes over a period of time.

Once the outline of the job has been established it is important to consider if the position needs to be filled at all. Employee requirements are constantly changing as the needs of the organisation develop and the employee will develop new skills and broaden his experience. Could the duties of the job be allocated to others or fulfilled by an alteration in operational procedures? If the job already exists and has expanded, perhaps now is the time to consider if it demands a higher level of skill or needs to be performed by more than one individual.

Internal versus external recruitment

Having resolved that the position is important and needs to be filled, the next decision is whether to fill it from within the organisation or recruit externally. The preferred solution is normally to identify a suitable candidate from within the organisation as this will not only save time and resources but will have the added benefit of improving internal morale and confidence. Some organisations have a unique culture, some utilise a defined technology and for these reasons it may be difficult to find an external recruit. Could the position be filled on a short-term basis or by a 'high flier' as part of a career development exercise?

Nevertheless, in some instances it may be necessary to recruit from outside so as to introduce new ideas or skills, thereby strengthening the organisation.

Before committing to the external recruitment route it is vital to establish if such personnel exist in the market place, and if so, can the organisation successfully attract such a person? These questions may be resolved in broad terms by contacting a relevant recruitment agency, a local Department of Employment office, other employers or by a review of recruitment advertisements in national newspapers. More definitive information can be obtained by reference to a salary survey or a relevant professional body.

Attracting a recruit to the organisation will be determined by four main factors: the nature of the position, its location, the remuneration package and the opportunities for future progression and development. The salary must be competitive with market rates but must also take account of the organisation's current wage or salary structure. Other benefits must also be competitive and provide an overall 'package' which is attractive. Offering in excess of market rates will attract many candidates, some of whom may be financially motivated only, offering too little will, conversely, produce a low standard of applicant. If it is not possible to offer market rates, then it will be necessary to redefine the position in order to arrive at a more representative level of responsibility, experience and expectation on the part of the applicant. It is critical to ensure that potential candidates are relevant to the job. Remuneration is also considered in this chapter in the context of retention.

Job description and personnel specifications

If the position is to be filled externally, and is likely to be attractive, then a detailed job description should be produced making use of the outline information gathered at the planning stage. Ideally the job description should include:

- the overall purpose of the job
- its place in the organisation structure
- the principal tasks, reponsibilities and duties
- resources available
- the interface with other parts of the organisation and external contracts
- any difficulties that the individual is likely to need to resolve.

The job description should not be prepared in isolation and if possible other relevant employees should be consulted in order to attempt to cover all aspects of the job.

Attention should also be focused on the individual specification which should follow logically from the completed job description. It is important to appreciate that the job to be performed should determine the candidate, and not vice versa, as many organisations continue to find to their cost. Many classifications of attributes can be used but they must focus on the job requirements in terms of skills, attitudes and abilities which can then be targeted during the selection process. A typical specification may include the following categories:

- *attainments*   Educational qualifications, skills and knowledge
- *intelligence*   Problem solving, ability to learn and flexible approach
- *aptitudes*   Specific or technical skills; languages
- *interests*   Motivational factors which relate to individual development or contribution
- *personality and character*   Behavioural traits
- *domestic and family circumstances*   Jobs affect private lives and vice versa
- *physical make-up*   Strength, stamina, etc.

A well prepared job description and specification will provide a sound basis for further recruitment action utilising either internal methods or assistance from external organisations.

Advertising

The principal means of soliciting applications for a vacancy are via advertising in appropriate media—press, radio or television. Here we will concentrate on recruitment advertising, as radio and television are expensive and are only appropriate for large scale multiple recruitment campaigns. Recruitment advertising is an increasingly complex area which creates significant costs and difficulties for the unwary; many organisations learn the hard lessons of advertising in a time consuming and expensive manner.

Recruitment advertising will continue to be an important integral part of the overall recruitment process and must be carefully considered and planned if it is to be effective. The advertisement relies heavily on the salient aspects of the job description and should be constructed in such a manner as to encourage a specific group of people to apply.

Ideally, the advertisment should attract a sufficient number of the most suitable candidates that are available either locally, nationally or internationally, so as to provide a range of candidates to fill the vacancy. A large response from a number of unsuitable candidates is a direct result of a poorly drafted or targeted advertisement. This will inevitably lead to wasteful administrative work and will hinder the recruitment process. The advertisement should ideally provide sufficient candidates to enable between eight and ten to be selected for initial consideration at the interview stage.

At the same time, the advertisement should discourage unsuitable candidates and represent the employing organisation in a favourable light without this becoming a pure public relations exercise. There are several basic guidelines which are straightforward to follow and provide the optimum prospect for success:

- the advertisement must be placed in the most appropriate publication, in the correct location and be well laid-out
- the title or heading must be clear and aimed at the required group of candidates
- the salary and location must be clearly indicated
- the copy should provide the salient information required by the candidate. It should not be excessive in length, clarity and economy of words being the hallmark of a well constructed advertisement
- clear instructions should be provided in order that candidates can respond.

Assistance can be provided by using a good advertising agency and the cost is normally included in any charge associated with the production of the finished artwork. If it is anticipated that recruitment advertisements will be run frequently it might be advantageous to cultivate a working relationship with a good local agency and this will also allow optimum use to be made of any specialist media knowledge and advice. This is important, as recruitment advertising is subject to many apparently illogical influencing factors, including aspects of fashion and trend. Normal guidelines for consumer advertising media do not apply in this respect and there is unfortunately no simple framework or set of guidelines to follow—the company should seek advice before commitment is made to producing and placing the advertisement.

Advertising rates vary enormously, depending upon the circulation of the publication, size and layout of the advertisement and seasonal fluctuations in the demand for advertising space. Either the publication's classified advertising department or an advertising agency will be able to provide accurate data on costs and relate this to the format of the proposed advertisement. Allowance should be made within the budget to cover the previously mentioned production costs.

Recruitment agencies and consultants

What other avenues are worth considering in the event that the organisation does not wish to advertise and/or handle the complete recruitment and selection process in-house? There are three main types of external recruitment service that should be considered—agencies, selection consultants and executive search consultants.

The number of recruitment agencies has grown substantially in recent years, especially in the computer systems, accountancy and secretarial sectors. Most advertise on their own behalf to attract candidates to match employers' requirements, some will conduct screening interviews and some will maintain a database of candidates. Agencies are normally used on the basis of their market sector knowledge and speed of response. They are particularly useful in filling clerical, secretarial and staff vacancies up to junior management levels.

The candidate databases maintained by some agencies offer a quick solution. However, in practice the candidate details are often outdated and there may be a time delay while the agency re-establishes contact with candidates to discuss the details of the position. In some cases, the quality of candidates may appear to be poor as good individuals seldom remain on a register for more than a short period of time. Registers can be helpful when an organisation has an on-going need for people with specialist skills or in the event that an advertisement has produced a poor response.

Selection consultants are often used in order to fill managerial and other senior appointments. There are many selection consultancies and they vary enormously in the quality of service that they provide and the calibre of consulting staff that they employ. These tend to handle all phases of the recruitment and selection process. The higher quality firms will advise on the position, the remuneration package, the employee specification and the best method of attracting good candidates. Candidates would be invited to apply to the consultancy who would then normally carry out screening and interviews in order to identify suitable candidates for shortlist consideration. The benefits are that senior management time will be saved and specialist expertise can be utilised. Selection consultants normally charge a fixed percentage of a candidate's starting salary which is often billed in stages and may not be contingent upon a successful appointment.

Executive search consultants, often referred to as 'Head Hunters', sometimes carry with them an aura of 'mystery', perhaps as the vacancies that they handle are never advertised and are filled as a direct result of careful research and direct approaches to suitable candidates. Executive search relies heavily on the identification of target companies where the best candidates are likely to be employed. Following this identification phase they then ascertain reputation and past performance before making a direct approach leading to interviews and the presentation of a shortlist. The use of search consultants is only really appropriate when the target list for potential candidates can be easily identified and the vacancy is at a senior managerial or board level. Fees vary but are typically based upon one-third of first year salary. Search can sometimes prove to be a costly and lengthy process due to the large amount of time-consuming research that is required and should therefore only be considered when advertising or selection is wholly inappropriate—for instance when the vacancy is particularly sensitive or confidential.

As a final comment on the use of agencies or consultants, it is always important to monitor closely their performance as the assignment progresses. It is also helpful to provide them with as much useful information as possible, concerning both the company and the relevant vacancy. This information can then be passed to candidates prior to interview.

It is beyond the scope of this chapter to go into further detail on other aspects of the selection process—interviewing, testing, making the final selection decision and following up. However, interviews which can be a bad predictor of suitability, should always be planned and only conducted by trained interviewers working to an established structure. Other selection methods such as psychometric assessment will assume even greater importance as the pool of potential candidates decreases and competition in the recruitment marketplace becomes more intense.

Remuneration and retention

Much effort and expense will be consumed by the recruitment process in the future. When considering the scenario where there are personnel and skills shortages it is even more important that recruitment activities are not increased or wasted as a result of the loss of key employees.

Remuneration is key factor which can provide a strong influence over retention, and many organisations are increasingly focused on the need to tailor remuneration packages to suit the needs of specific employees. Too often the main consideration for the retention of staff has been a matter of cash. The importance of the basic salary should not be under-estimated but it is now even more relevant to consider a flexible and commercial approach to improve the motivation and loyalty of employees. However, this flexibility must obviously not be at the expense of cost effectiveness for the employer.

Organisations must consider remuneration packages in the widest context and ask questions such as:

- what are competitors offering in terms of salary and other benefits?
- are the terms and conditions of employment relevant to the market place?
- how often are salary reviews conducted, and what criteria are used?
- is there a bonus scheme and could it motivate employees?
- if appropriate, is there a share scheme for employees?
- have incentives or performance related pay been considered?
- is the pension scheme considered as part of the overall remuneration package and how does it compare with others?
- is the most made of the company car scheme?
- are the right cars being allocated to various levels of staff and managers when compared with other companies?
- is the relocation scheme suitable in the light of the current economic situation and housing market?

Considering a response to these and other related questions will assist in the development of alternatives or extensions to the more 'traditional' remuneration policy, some of which are now covered in greater depth.

Flexible remuneration

In recent years there has been a trend towards a greater range of innovative and flexible benefits, such as maternity/paternity leave, low-interest loans, 'golden hellos', opportunities to work from home and childcare allowances.

In addition to the more 'novel' incentives, some organisations have introduced the concept of flexible remuneration with a number of key elements being offered within a pre-determined package for employees. This concept allows individuals to choose from a remuneration 'menu' to suit their specific needs. A younger married person may opt to take a higher basic salary to reduce a large mortgage, a young single person may opt to have an expensive company car at the expense of a lower salary, while an older individual may value increased pension contributions and savings plans. Such schemes are more relevant to some industries and organisational cultures than others and require careful planning if they are to achieve the desired objective of improved retention.

Performance related pay

A further means of enhancing the remuneration package is to introduce a scheme which links an element of the salary, or salary increase, to individual performance. Such schemes, which are growing in number, utilise the central concept of strengthening the link between pay and performance as a means of motivation. If used to full effect this can also remove the established concept of a company-wide annual pay increase and relates increases directly to performance, position in a salary range and the available budget.

In practice, such schemes tend to be more relevant to management levels and should be linked to an annual appraisal or objective-setting exercise which in turn monitors individual performance. If properly structured the scheme can relate salary increases to contribution and lead to an improvement in overall company performance. However, the organisation must also recognise and be able to cope with the situation where a bad or poor performer does not receive an increase in a particular review period. The appraisal scheme element will only be successful if widespread training for appraisers is undertaken.

Bonus or profit sharing schemes

Profit sharing or bonus schemes can also form part of an effective remuneration package as an aid to retention. These tend to be used either on a company-wide basis or for a small group of senior managers or directors. When used throughout an organisation the amount that an individual receives tends to be allocated from a pool which is based upon profit performance. Usually, a poor financial performance on the part of the organisation results in no profit share or bonus being paid and this could be considered as having a negative or de-motivating effect.

At the senior level such schemes tend to realise more substantial amounts and can be related either to overall financial performance or that of the manager or director's own function or area of responsibility.

In both cases there are important tax considerations (as outlined in Chapter 4) and strict Inland Revenue guidelines which will require specialist advice prior to implementation.

Training and development

Training and development initiatives can also have an important positive effect on retaining, motivating and attracting employees. Recently more attention has been focused on this area after much neglect in the late 1970s and early 1980s. Realistic career development and training plans may achieve a great deal in providing employees with an incentive to remain and progress within the organisation.

Internal training activity should take advantage of external assistance including that provided by government bodies, eg the Training Agency and Employment service, where valuable training support and grants are available. Consideration should also be given to the training of young people who will provide a valuable source of ready-made, in-house skills and knowledge upon completion of their training. In this connection efforts should also be made to cultivate links with local schools, colleges and, if appropriate, universities.

Conclusion

Recruitment and retention will develop into major determinants of company performance in the future as the shortage of key skills becomes increasingly pronounced. Many growing organisations have developed their strategies based upon careful manpower planning and innovative personnel policies which will allow them to recruit, retain and develop staff in order to meet their business needs. They are therefore in a position to gain substantial benefits as a result.

The aspects of human resources discussed in this chapter do not necessarily require a large personnel department, or even a personnel manager, to plan and develop. However, elements of specialist assistance may be required in the initial implementation phase. In addition, although the responsibility for effective personnel management rests with the line manager, and not with a separate personnel function, the complex area of human resources is becoming increasingly crucial to business success. The future of the personnel activity will move further towards a pro-active, enabling and assisting role, rather than the more traditional administrative and policing activity. The links between directors, line managers and personnel professionals will need to strengthen if companies are to maximise future business opportunities.

Of all the resources employed by the growing company, the effective management of personnel is one of the fundamentals to the continued success of the business. The initial step is the development of a manpower plan; choosing the right calibre of staff in the first place is key to the formation of a winning team.

The skill shortages forecast for the 1990s bring into sharp focus the need to concentrate on the retention of existing staff and the adoption of a flexible remuneration policy is clearly a major factor in attracting and retaining employees loyal to the business.

Earlier chapters have stressed the need to involve employees in the planning process and to keep them informed of the corporate objectives so that they are clearly aware of how their efforts contribute to the fulfilment of the company's strategy. This principle will of course still be true if employees are 'recruited' as a result of an aquisition of another organisation. In the next chapter we discuss this and other factors which must be considered in the development of an aquisitions strategy.

CHAPTER 8

Building on Growth

Introduction

Typically, the early growth achieved by many private companies will have been organic; that is to say, development has been achieved internally by, for example, launching new products, entering new markets and increasing, by improved quality, advertising and publicity, the company's market share.

Indeed the analysis in this book, with regard to marketing and managing production systems, has been aimed principally at those companies experiencing organic growth. In this chapter we introduce the concept that organic growth may be supplemented by corporate acquisitions.

Chapter 1 emphasised the need to develop a corporate (or 'business') plan. The business plan should identify the strengths and weaknesses of the company whereby a strategy may be developed to build on the strengths and diminish any weaknesses. Moreover, the business plan should highlight any external opportunities for growth and any factors which may threaten management's plan for growth. Such opportunities and threats could be exploited or allayed in several ways, including: joint venture arrangements, corporate venturing, licensing agreements, franchising, further organic growth or acquisitions.

The greatest advantage of using acquisitions to enhance growth, in preference to the alternatives above, is the speed with which growth can result following the acquisition.

In Chapter 3 we discussed the possibility of a public flotation as a long- or medium-term objective. If this course of action is followed it is inevitable that the pressure to extend the growth curve will increase as the company is increasingly accountable to a wider shareholder base. Again, growth may be accelerated by corporate acquisition. However, if the shareholders of the purchaser are to be fully satisfied with the performance of the new group it is critical that an acquisitions strategy is developed to ensure that this path is followed in a co-ordinated and considered fashion.

The following topics will be covered and these are intended as a guide to the development of an acquisitions strategy and to the considerations necessary when carrying out a valuation of a potential target company:

1. reasons for acquiring another company
2. identifying the characteristics of an ideal target
3. the acquisitions team
4. identifying specific targets
5. valuation of target companies
6. investigation of the target
7. post-acquisition considerations.

Reasons for acquiring another company

The most common rationale for a takeover is to *improve existing market share*. Not only should the new group benefit from a merged customer base, but also the target company may have a superior distribution network or marketing capability. Conversely, the acquiring company may have an advantage in these areas, compared to the target, although it perceives an opportunity to develop the target company's immature products using its own established resources so that a *synergistic benefit* results.

Alternatively, the target may be in a different market sector which provides an opportunity for the acquiring company to (adapt, and then) sell its own products in that market and thereby *expand the target market*. The simplest example of this occurs when an overseas subsidiary is acquired in order to exploit a foreign market.

It may be the case that the acquiring company could utilise the *advanced technical skills* of the target company (or vice versa) to improve its product range and thereby increase potential for growth.

The technical *skills of the target company management* may be in areas not directly linked to product development, such as marketing, sales or operations management. The target company's management may have performed to a higher level in some areas, compared with the acquiring company's management, and so the acquisition may be justified in the anticipation that the acquiring company will benefit from the superior skills acquired in these areas. Conversely, the target company could have real market potential whilst suffering from weak management that should be replaced following acquisition.

In addition, *economies of scale*, such as enhanced purchasing power, production efficiency improvements may result from the takeover.

Finally, so called 'conglomerate' acquisitions have been made to *improve financial structure and reported returns*. The strategy behind a number of conglomerate acquisitions follows that illustrated in the product portfolio chart detailed in Chapter 1 (Fig 1.5 on page 11). 'Cash Cow' subsidiaries are balanced by 'Wildcats', who eventually became 'Stars' or are harvested (the 'Stars' are the 'Cash Cows' of the future). A significant difficulty with conglomerate organisations is that the companies in the group are often based in a range of diverse industries such that it is problematical for central management to control and contribute to their continued development.

Identifying the characteristics of an ideal target

Once the rationale for an acquisitions strategy has been decided upon and agreed, management should then construct a checklist of acceptable characteristics to produce an ideal pro-forma for a potential acquisition. The desirable characteristics will vary depending on the specific goals of the acquisitive company, but will often be measured within the following parameters:

1. the maximum acquisition price that the acquiror is willing or able to pay

2. the acceptable means of payment
3. the level of financial and management investment required in the target, following acquisition so as to enable it to realise its potential
4. the market share held by the target
5. the range of products sold by the target
6. the relative size of the target
7. the market sector and location of the target
8. profitability
9. the cash flow profile of the target.

In considering 4, 6 and 7 above regarding the market share, size and sector the company may need to bear in mind the limits imposed by merger controls in the UK and any foreign government controls where the target is based overseas.

The acquisition team

Having decided upon the characteristics of an ideal target company the management should construct a team of specialists from inside and external to the firm. It is advisable to appoint an overall project leader to guide and co-ordinate the acquisition through each stage. The person appointed should be senior, experienced and qualified to enable him to deal with all relevant parties at all stages. The project leader will initially manage the research phase identifying potential targets who fit the key characteristics sought. An accountant will be required to investigate and report upon the target companies. In addition tax advisors, actuaries to advise on pension schemes, solicitors, surveyors and other valuation experts will be required as part of the due diligence process that is so often critical in uncovering potential problem areas.

If the target company is a public company the team may also include public relations and advertising consultants, stockbrokers and a merchant bank.

Moreover, a senior member of the management team should be identified to manage, monitor and control the new acquisition once the purchase is completed.

Identifying specific targets

The management of the company will inevitably have their own ideas of potential targets through knowledge of the industry (if a target in the same industry is sought). Moreover, sales or purchasing department personnel may be a valuable source of information on potential targets from their contacts with customers and suppliers.

In addition, the company's professional advisors and management's other business contacts should be able to assist in identifying potential targets.

Relevant trade literature such as directories, catalogues, journals and surveys will also provide leads.

Finally, other sources of information on potential targets include the following:

1. published accounts

2. Extel cards
3. McCarthy cards
4. financial press
5. credit rating information from credit agencies.

Once the initial investigation has been performed, and potential targets identified, these can be matched against the ideal characteristics checklist to eliminate any companies not worthy of further consideration.

Valuation of target companies

In reaching a valuation on any target company, so as to form the basis for the initial offer, it is important to understand several basic principles which prevail in the valuation process. The first is that value is the price which the purchaser will pay and the vendor will accept. In transactions, value is determined by negotiation and arises in a particular place at a particular time and in particular circumstances. Moreover, there may be special circumstances affecting a valuation:

- the target may provide synergy with the existing business
- the acquisition may lead to the elimination of competition or excess industry capacity
- the acquisition could provide a cost effective means of entering a new market
- the target company may be in financial or managerial difficulty.

The presence of these circumstances ensures that valuation is not a mechanical application of formulae but rather an exercise in judgement and negotiation.

Various formulae may be used as useful tools, although it is rare that any single formula could be regarded as the sole factor that is relevant. All factors must be taken into account to a greater or lesser extent. In addition, any examples of similar businesses that have changed hands recently are important indicators of potential value.

The overriding principle for all company valuations is that the value of a business relates to the future expectations of the buyer and it is based upon, or is related to, what the target business can earn or realise.

A primary factor in determining the amount a corporate or private investor should be prepared to pay for an investment is the rate of return required by that investor.

The rate of return consists of a 'risk free' rate (eg gilts, etc) plus a premium determined by the risk inherent in the investment. Risk in itself is subjective but can normally be associated with uncertainty—uncertainty in the market, uncertainty of future earnings, etc. This is difficult to quantify and will largely depend on the views and expectations of the individual investor. It is crucial, however, that risk is considered by the valuer in determining final value.

The preliminary value of a company on an earnings basis, excluding any growth in earnings, can be determined by the following formula.

$$\text{Value} = \frac{\text{Maintainable earnings}}{\text{Required rate of return}}$$

For example, where maintainable earnings (post tax) are estimated at £100 and the investor's required rate of return is 12.5%, the value would equate to £800.

The same value is more often derived by converting the rate of return into its reciprocal multiple (or price earnings ratio) and then multiplying this by maintainable post tax profits. Thus, in the above example, the multiple or price earnings ratio ('p/e') would equate to 8, which when applied to maintainable earnings of £100 results in a value of £800.

The use of quoted p/e's to value unquoted businesses has become common practice in recent years. The p/e achieved by a quoted company is based on the current share price and the company's most recent reported earnings. The use of quoted company p/e's can be useful, but one must consider that they normally represent small shareholder transactions only, at prices which are often influenced by institutional buyers, international events, speculation and takeovers. Consequently, quoted shares may have little in common with the value of an unquoted company and so their p/e ratios should be viewed with caution.

In addition to the potential maintainable profits, the purchaser should also consider any redundant or surplus assets which could be realised and thereby increase the amount the purchaser may be willing to pay for the target.

In summary, for a business as a whole (that is, a 100% shareholding), valuation is usually based upon three factors:

1. best estimate of future maintainable earnings (FME)
2. application of an appropriate rate of return/multiple to those earnings to provide an earnings based valuation (p/e multiplied by FME)
3. surplus assets.

Each of these factors is now discussed in more detail.

Maintainable earnings

The purchaser needs to assess future maintainable earnings as a basis for considering the attraction of a potential acquisition. In making this assessment, the purchaser will normally have available the historic results of the target as well as forecasts prepared by the management of the target.

HISTORIC OR FORECAST PROFITS?

Historic profits are only relevant in so far as they are a guide to future profits. Historic profits are generally used as they have certain advantages over forecasts in that they are:

- *readily available* Companies or businesses for sale should have accounts available
- *certain* Annual accounts will be available which are based on actual historic figures and will be accompanied by an audit report
- *easily analysed* Explanations can be sought for trends and variations.

Forecasts suffer from the corresponding disadvantages:

- *not always available* Many private companies do not have even basic budgeting or forecasting procedures

- *potentially unreliable*   Forecasts are inherently subjective and liable to significant variation; many companies have a history of inaccurate forecasting
- *reliant on assumptions*   Additional uncertainties exist due to factors outside of the directors' control.

Moreover, initial budgets and forecasts are often prepared by vendors, who have a vested interest by indicating high future profits and the forecasts may suffer from over-optimism.

Historic profits   If past results are to be used as a basis for estimating future maintainable earnings, it is important that adjustments are made to reflect the fact that some factors, which were relevant in the past, may no longer apply once the acquisition is complete, and to eliminate non-recurring income or expenditure. The following are examples of typical adjustments which may be necessary:

- directors' remuneration—this is a common adjustment to reflect the market cost of directors' services, and is often necessary where owner-directors have previously withdrawn a substantial proportion of trading profit as remuneration
- if premises are not being sold with the business, notional market rental should be allowed for in place of depreciation
- income from, and costs of, surplus assets should be eliminated if those assets are to be valued separately
- interest receivable and payable adjustments may also be necessary to allow for restructuring (eg pre-disposal dividend) or excessive debt
- finally the tax charge may need to be recalculated to reflect the likely future effective tax rate.

Forecast earnings   The following factors are relevant when considering the use of forecasts to estimate future maintainable earnings.

- available forcasts are useful since a valuation requires an understanding of estimated future results, as this may differ from past experience
- forecasts should, however, be treated with caution, especially if they show a sudden change in profitability
- the acquiror should review the past budgeting and forecasting history of the target and consider whether it has been sufficiently accurate for any reliance to be placed
- the acquiror should be satisfied that the forecasts take account of all known changes in trading conditions
- the acquiror should decide whether to make an adjustment to reflect any uncertainties in maintainable earnings or in the price earnings multiple.

Profit trends   Any profit trends shown by historic or forecast results should be taken into account when estimating future maintainable earnings.

The estimate of future maintainable earnings may be based on just one year's earnings or over several years. If the latter is used the acquiror may need to take an average figure. Averaging is most appropriate where the target has an uneven profit record. The average should probably not be based on historic results which are more than five years old. Weighting may also be appropriate to give more significance to more recent results. The purchaser should also consider the inclusion of forecast results on the calculation of average maintainable earnings.

The difficulty with using an average, especially where complex weighting formulae are used, is that it gives a doubtful accuracy to the estimate of maintainable earnings simply because it is derived from a calculation. It should be remembered that the estimate of maintainable earnings is subjective. In addition, several estimates should be made using different bases before a final result is determined.

Rate of return and the price earnings ratio

A foundation from which a rate can be derived is from information relating to other similar company acquisitions. However, this information should be assessed with care to ensure that situations are comparable.

If no such information is available the acquiror may need to use published p/e's as a guide:

- a limited number of public companies should be identified that have similar characteristics to the one being valued
- the purchaser should examine all available information in relation to these companies to ascertain any special factors that may have affected their market price
- the purchaser will need to adjust the quoted p/e's for deficiencies inherent in them such as:
  —they are calculated on historical profits, and may be seriously distorted by investors' present assessments of the trends of profits
  —they represent minority holdings.

The valuation will need to be refined by considering the following:

- the effect of a range of p/e ratios above and below that originally selected
- the effect of a range of estimated net maintainable profits above and below the range originally selected
- the effect of any delay there may be in achieving the estimated maintainable earnings
- generally, for a given level of business activity, the higher the estimated net maintainable profits the greater the risk that they will not be achieved. Greater risk will require a higher rate of return and a lower p/e
- the tangible asset backing. A high tangible asset backing may indicate a lower risk which could result in a higher p/e
- the valuations which could be obtained by valuing the separate businesses within the company
- the amount which could be realised on a forced liquidation. Such an amount would normally represent the minimum value
- the valuation must avoid double counting. For example, if maintainable earnings are discounted because of uncertainty, one should not *also* take a lower p/e to reflect the same uncertainty
- undisclosed liabilities.

All the above factors will lead the valuer to adopt a narrow range of p/e's within which to assess the value of the business on an earnings basis.

Surplus assets

To the earnings based valuation must be added surplus assets. The balance sheet of the target company should be examined for those assets that are excess to the company's requirements and are capable of realisation. These could include:

- excess cash
- a portfolio of readily realisable investments
- investment in excess land, buildings and equipment
- unutilised licences, franchises, copyrights and patents.

The possibility that such assets do not appear in the balance sheet, or are included at considerably less than their realisable value should also be considered and independent valuations may be made where appropriate.

Other considerations

Loss making companies   These can be very difficult to value. It could be said that if there are no earnings there is no value other than the break-up value of the assets. In fact, many loss making companies are sold for substantial sums. They are, however, more difficult to value in isolation than profitable companies. The attractions of loss making companies include:

- rationalisation of operations with the purchaser's existing operations
- elimination of competition
- availability of assets at a discount.

In all cases, there must be a belief in future profitability, if only through better management, or enhancement of profitability of existing operations.

The valuation from the purchaser's viewpoint relies on his assessment of future profits. Historic losses are of no value other than as a base for profit improvement. The assessment should include detailed proposals of any rationalisation, redundancies or interim losses. There should also be a discount for the risk that a turn-around will not be achieved in the timescale envisaged (or at all) and an allowance for the direct costs of implementation should be made. The valuation can then be made on the basis of an appropriate p/e multiple, allowing for the fact that profits may not be earned for some time.

Finally, during the negotiation phase, management should beware of passing on to the vendor the advantages which the purchaser can bring to the business although these may be obvious.

Net assets basis of valuation   Net assets are not generally considered to be a prime consideration in determining value other than for pure asset-based entities such as property or securities investment companies.

However, some consideration is usually given, even if the main value is arrived at on the earnings basis. In theory, the earnings basis should be sufficient, but some regard to assets may give comfort to the overall valuation.

The acquiror should be aware of potentially valuable assets not recorded such as leases or surplus assets.

The difference between assets acquired at their fair value and the fair value of the consideration is goodwill. Many purchasers, having valued on an earnings basis, do this calculation as a check on the reasonableness of the result by reference to the resultant goodwill. They will then consider whether the amount paid for goodwill is excessive given the nature of the business.

Normally one expects higher goodwill with a service orientated business than a manufacturing concern with its greater volume of fixed assets. However, such acquisitions are potentially more risky as the prime asset is often its staff who tend to be somewhat more mobile than an item of plant and equipment.

Large minority/majority holdings What is large depends on the circumstances, what matters is the degree of influence:

- *substantial or dominant minority holdings* Minority holdings that, whilst not exercising in their own right more than 50% of the voting powers, nevertheless often exercise significant or dominant influence over the company's affairs
- *majority holdings* Holdings that can exercise over 50% of the voting powers and so can substantially influence the company's affairs

For these shareholdings the acquiror will place the major emphasis on future earnings and available profits.

- *controlling holdings* holdings that can exercise over 75% of the voting powers and so can control the company's affairs.

For these holdings the purchaser will place the major emphasis on either future earnings or asset realisation, depending on which produces the greater value.

With all holdings the acquiror needs to consider his ability either to realise the investment or to control or influence a future take-over or flotation.

Pension funds Pension funds are not assets of the company. A detailed examination of pension fund considerations is beyond the scope of this book. It is important to note, however, that over-funded pension schemes may give benefit to the acquiror. It should also be noted that a social security bill is currently passing through Parliament which may limit the benefit arising on a particular scheme.

Investigation of the target

A detailed investigation of the target company is usually possible when the bid is uncontested and involves a private company.

The investigation work should cover the following:

1. confirm that the target matches the ideal characteristics identified by the acquiring company

2. establish the reasons behind the contention that the target company is for sale or is vulnerable to take-over. Confirm that there are no negative factors which will be difficult to overcome post acquisition
3. review the style of management of the target and morale of staff employed by the target
4. identify any trends in performance which may impact on future profitability
5. investigate the reasons for any unexplained increases in sales and profitability in the company's recent history.

There is a need to investigate and analyse the business and the trading results as closely as possible and any investigation into a target company's potential should deal first with historic profits as an indicator of future maintainable earnings.

In an agreed private purchase, it is usual to have some access to the company and its management; the main restrictive factor on pre-acquisition access is confidentiality.

Some suggested (but not exhaustive) areas for investigation are:

1. Nature of business
   - products and market
   - trends in the business
   - competitors and market share
   - rate of technological change

2. Sources of profit
   - analysis by product/product line
   - major customers or contracts
   - effect of introduction of new products

3. Net assets and surplus assets
   - does the company own or rent premises?
   - recent capital expenditure and future investment required
   - assets surplus to trading requirements

4. 'Non-core' business
   - are there peripheral activities?
   - could they be sold off?

5. Management
   - quality
   - experience

6. Level of directors' remuneration
   - salary
   - expenses
   - pension contributions

7. Liabilities
   - taxation
   - contingent.

The investigator should, inter alia, look at the quality of the financial information provided by the target as this will reveal useful information on the quality of the management control systems. Moreover, he should look to the systems themselves, the accounting policies used in the accounts and the environment in which they were prepared in order to make an assessment of the quality of the available figures.

Post acquisition considerations

If the reason for the acquisition is to obtain synergy through, for example, improved efficiency or market expansion, then a valuation of the target based upon historic results only is not likely to give a complete picture and may result in an incorrect and expensive investment decision.

The acquisition team must take a wider view and make an assessment of the likely market and operational benefits of the takeover before attempting to predict the financial outcome of the acquisition. This assessment should reinforce the rationale for the acquisition, identify and eliminate any redundant resources and provide an action plan to achieve the perceived benefits of the takeover—the post acquisition plan.

The need for an acquisition strategy, which includes the development of a post acquisition plan, is highlighted during the negotiation period as the target company will often lose close management direction and opportunities may be foregone in a period of uncertainty. In addition, the target management team, who were perhaps seen as one of the benefits of the takeover, may feel uncomfortable in the face of this uncertainty and desert the company. The post acquistition plan should therefore aim to give the new management reassurance that the takeover can be of benefit to their company and themselves personally, as well as providing a set of objectives against which to monitor the future performance of the group. These objectives will ultimately be translated into budgets and business plans for the acquiring and the target company.

It is particularly important, if the acquiror wishes to retain the target management team, that they are involved in the preparation of these plans. In addition, the budgets should be reviewed regularly by the person appointed by the acquiror to monitor the performance of the new subsidiary.

Conclusion

Some basic considerations for managing organic growth have been analysed in this book. These same rules apply to the development of an acquisitions strategy and the management of new companies brought into the group. The fundamental principles of planning, implementation, monitoring and controlling the business are paramount to the continued successful growth of the business.

Calculation of the Minimum Equity Stake Which a Venture Capital Fund Must Take to Achieve its Target IRR— a Simple Example

This example assumes that XYZ Ltd is just starting up and it forecasts that by its fourth year (when the venture capital firm wishes to exit from the investment) it will earn profits of £500,000 after tax. Suppose, further, that the initial funding request is £300,000 and that the venture capital fund requires a 40% compound rate of return on its investment. (NOTE: Because business plans are often optimistic, venture capital firms will frequently make a 'risk adjustment' to the pricing calculation by reducing either the forecast after tax earnings or the earnings multiple.)

One method used to determine how the equity may be allocated is as follows:

1. The venture capital firm will estimate the value of the company in the fourth year based on a multiple of earnings for similar companies. Assume that, based on the venture capital firm's research of the industry, companies similar to XYZ Ltd are selling for approximately 15 times current earnings. Then a discounted multiple of say 10 might be used for forecast earnings. This would give the company a total valuation in year 4 of £5,000,000 (10 x £500,000 profits).

2. The 'present value' of the company can then be calculated as follows:

$$\text{Present value} = \frac{\text{future valuation}}{(1 + i)^n}$$

where the future valuation is the amount calculated in paragraph 1 of this example.

i = venture capital firm's required rate of return.
n = number of years until the date of the forecast earnings used in calculating the future valuation.

The present value of XYZ Ltd would be calculated as follows:

$$\text{Present value} = \frac{\text{future valuation}}{(1 + i)^n}$$

$$= \frac{£5,000,000}{(1 + 0.4)^4}$$

$$= \frac{£5,000,000}{3.8416}$$

$$= £1,300,000 \text{ (approx)}$$

3. Based on the initial required funding of £300,000, the venture capital firm's share of the company must be at least 23%, if it is to achieve its target rate of return on this investment.

$$\text{Share of company} = \frac{\text{Initial funding}}{\text{Present value}}$$

$$= \frac{£300,000}{£1,300,000}$$

$$= 23\%$$

The table below shows the differences in the venture capital firm's share, if the earnings multiples and the required rates of return over a four year period were varied for XYZ Ltd.

Venture capital firm's required % ownership

Earnings multiple	Required rate of return			
	30%	40%	50%	60%
5	34	46	61	79
10	17	23	30	39
15	11	15	20	26

Not all venture capital firms will use the methods and the formulae used above, and they apply only to straight equity investments. They are provided here only as a guide to help you evaluate your company's worth to venture capital firms.

The following table of present value factors, $(1+i)^n$, can be used in calculating the pricing structure.

Present value factors

Years	Required rate of return			
	30%	40%	50%	60%
1	1.3	1.4	1.5	1.6
2	1.7	2.0	2.3	2.6
3	2.2	2.7	3.4	4.1
4	2.9	3.8	5.1	6.6
5	3.7	5.4	7.6	10.5

APPENDIX B

Grants

- *Enterprise Zones* A list of current Enterprise Zones in the UK is appended.

  The incentives for businesses operating within these areas are as follows:

  —full exemption from rates on industrial and commercial property
  —full exemption from levies by Industrial Training Boards
  —100% capital allowances for expenditure on industrial and commercial buildings.

  The grants are awarded by the Department of the Environment and are available to new and existing industrial and commercial enterprises.

- *Regional selective assistance* These are project-related grants for industrial and commercial projects which bring a regional or national benefit and create or sustain employment in Development areas or Intermediate areas. Generally, all non-revenue items of expenditure are eligible; for example:

  —purchase of land
  —site preparation
  —buildings, plant and machinery.

  The grants are awarded by the Department of Trade and Industry. The size of the award will depend upon the circumstances of the proposed project and the level of regional and national benefit that will accrue from it. The grant received will be taxable as a trading receipt.

- *Inner urban areas* Within Great Britain certain areas have been designated as 'Improvement areas'. A list of these areas is appended. Loans and grants are available to businesses for environmental improvement and the modification or improvement of industrial or commercial buildings. This assistance is intended to encourage projects that might otherwise not have proceeded.

  Where the assistance is in respect of environmental improvement, up to 100% of the cost may be eligible for a grant. Where assistance is for the modification or improvement of buildings the grant is restricted to 50% of the cost.

  The grants are generally awarded by the relevant local authorities who will exercise discretion as to the level of the grant which in turn will be dependent upon the value of the project to the area.

- *City Grant Scheme* This scheme is designed to support business investment that benefits 'rundown' urban areas in England. These areas are shown at the end of this appendix. To be eligible, projects must:

—provide jobs
—provide private housing and benefits
—exceed £200,000 in value
—require public assistance to proceed.

Essentially the City Grant Scheme bridges the gap between the cost of the project to the business and the value of the project upon completion to the community. In the case of a housing development the value could be the capitalised rents of the completed dwellings.

Applications should be made to the Department of the Environment Regional Office responsible for the urban area.

- *Government factories*   A wide range of factory premises are available for lease or sale to manufacturing and service businesses operating in Development and Intermediate areas in Great Britain. Rent is normally charged at commercial rates and is subject to regular review. Smaller work units are also available with on-site management, support and common services. These units are normally available on flexible letting arrangements, enabling fast growth businesses to accommodate the units for relatively short periods before they 'outgrow' the space.

  Applications should be made to:

—English Estates in England
—Scottish Development Agency
—Welsh Development Agency.

- *European Investment Bank Loans*   The European Investment Bank (EIB) offers loan financing on flexible terms for specific fixed capital investment projects undertaken by businesses in certain areas. Loans are related to asset life and may be for:

—capital investment in infrastructure
—transport
—telecommunications
—energy
—industry
—tourism.

  The private sector business must fulfil the following criteria to qualify for consideration:

—the project must cost between £2 and £13 million
—the net assets of the business must be less than £50 million
—the business must have less than 500 employees.

  Loans are available on up to 50% of the gross investment cost, including related working capital increases. The EIB will normally insist upon either corporate or third party support as security for the facility.

  The interest costs of these loans are near to the EIB's cost of borrowings. Repayment of principal and interest is normally made in equal six monthly instalments in arrears. Repayment holidays of up to five years are available.

- *The DTI Enterprise Initiative*   This is a self-help package offered to UK businesses, under which the Department of Trade and Industry pays up to half the costs of between 5 to 15 days consultancy advice; the following initiatives are available:

—marketing
—design
—quality
—manufacturing
—business planning
—financial & information systems
—export
—research & technology
—business education.

- *Training schemes*   The government provides a number of training incentive schemes aimed at a wide range of businesses. Grants are available of up to £30,000 per company against the cost of training. The company is most likely to receive assistance if:

  —it is a small company
  —training is likely to have a significant impact on the business
  —the firm has little or no experience of training.

- *Urban Development Corporations (UDC)*   There are currently seven UDC's nationwide, which are sometimes linked to Enterprise zones. The UDC's usually provide cheaper factory/office accommodation, and various grants.

- *Rural Development Areas (RDA)*   There are 28 RDA's in England which cover some 35% of the country, the aid is normally in the form of loans or grants of up to £75,000, however there are a number of smaller schemes aimed at training and business development aspects.

- There are many other forms of assistance in the form of grants and loans, which it is beyond the scope of this book to explore in detail. However, listed below are a few of the other schemes:

  —British (and European) coal and steel Enterprises offer grants and loans to businesses that are expanding in traditional coal and steel industry areas, and in so doing relieving the unemployment originally caused by closures
  —transport grants of up to 50% are available to businesses utilising rail freight facilities in an effort to make greater use of the rail system
  —assistance is available to businesses engaged in the tourist industry through various tourist boards. Finance will only be given if the project is genuinely enhancing off-season tourism, encouraging visitors to less traditional locations, attracting overseas visitors or creating employment.

Enterprise Zones

England

Corby
Dudley
Glanford
Hartlepool
Isle of Dogs
Middlesborough
N.E. Lancashire
N.W. Kent
Rotherham
Salford
Scunthorpe
Speke
Telford
Trafford
Tyneside
Wakefield
Wellingborough
Workington

Scotland

Clydebank
Invergordon
Tayside

Wales

Delyn
Lower Swansea Valley
Milford Haven Waterway

N. Ireland

Belfast
Londonderry

Improvement areas (only designated in Great Britain)

England

* Barnsley
* Birmingham
* Blackburn
* Bolton
* Bradford
* Brent
* Coventry
* Doncaster
  Ealing
* Gateshead
* Greenwich
* Hackney
* Hammersmith and Fulham
* Haringay
* Hartlepool
* Islington

* Kingston upon Hull
* Knowsley
* Lambeth
* Langbaurgh
* Leeds
* Leicester
* Lewisham
* Liverpool
* Manchester
* Middlesborough
* Newcastle-upon-Tyne
* Newham
* North Tyneside
* Nottingham
* Oldham
* Rochdale
* Rotherham
* St Helens
* Salford
* Sefton
* Sheffield
* South Tyneside
* Southwark
* Sunderland
* Tower Hamlets
* Walsall
* Wigan
* Wirral
* Wolverhampton

Scotland

Clydebank
City of Dundee
Dumbarton
City of Glasgow
Hamilton
Inverclyde
Monklands
Motherwell
Renfrew

Wales

Blaenau Gwent
Cardiff
Cynon Valley
Merthyr Tydfil
Newport
Ogwr

Port Talbot
Rhondda
Rhymney Valley
Swansea

Urban programme areas

All improvement areas marked *
and additionally:

Bristol
Derby
Dudley
Halton
Kensington and Chelsea
Kirklees
Plymouth
Preston
Stockton-on-Tees
Wandsworth
The Wrekin

PAYE Considerations

Your questions answered

Compliance

WHAT ARE MY RESPONSIBILITIES AS AN EMPLOYER?

The PAYE regulations are set out in Statutory Instrument 1973/No 334 entitled The Income Tax (Employments) Regulations 1973. In addition the Inland Revenue publish an *Employer's Guide to PAYE* which covers the main areas of the PAYE system and lists those payments which have to be treated as pay for PAYE purposes. It also gives detailed information about what to do in particular cases. The guide itself has no legal force and in cases of doubt reference should be made to the regulations themselves.

The employer's responsibilities are set out in Section A4 of the *Employer's Guide* and are reproduced below:

- you must operate PAYE even if an employee claims he does not come within the system, perhaps because he says he pays tax as a self-employed person or as a listed company. In fact you should operate PAYE if you are in any doubt at all about any of the people that you take on. Get in touch with your Tax Office and keep on operating PAYE unless the Tax Office tells you to stop
- if you do not operate PAYE when you are meant to you may:
—have to pay the Inland Revenue the tax you should have deducted from the payments you have made to your employees.
—be liable to interest and/or penalties.

At the end of the tax year the employer must send the Inspector details of employees' expenses and benefits provided in the year. The forms to be used for this are P11D and P9D.

WHAT PAYMENTS ARE COVERED BY THE PAYE SYSTEM AND WHEN IS PAYMENT DUE TO THE INLAND REVENUE?

The *Employer's Guide to PAYE* (Section A3) sets out the payments which are to be treated as pay for tax deduction purposes. These include the following:

Earnings	Perks	Round sum expenses
Salaries	Honoraria	allowances
Wages	Sick pay	Payments from profit

Fees	Statutory sick pay	Holiday pay
Overtime	Maternity pay	Certain other
Bonuses	Statutory maternity	expenses payments
Commission	pay	
Pensions	Vouchers that can be	
	exchanged for cash	
	sharing schemes	

The PAYE tax and national insurance contributions due for a tax month should be paid by the 19th of the following month.

WHEN WOULD I NEED TO OPERATE PAYE FOR EMPLOYEES ASSIGNED TO WORK AT OUR OFFICES IN THE UK BY A FOREIGN EMPLOYER?

PAYE must be operated for:

- all employees working at a UK branch or office of an overseas business, and
- all employees, including directors, who work under the general control and management of a business in the UK. This is the case whether the person is paid by the UK concern or by the overseas concern. The PAYE regulations can make the UK concern liable for PAYE where this has not been properly accounted for.

FOR WHICH EMPLOYEES DO I NEED TO SUBMIT A P11D?

A P11D return should be submitted to the Inland Revenue for the following individuals:

- all directors, with the exception of certain full-time working directors and directors of non-profit making organisations or charities whose emoluments do not exceed the P11D threshold. We refer to these employees as 'higher-paid employees'
- employees whose emoluments exceed the P11D threshold.

The P11D threshold is currently £8,500, and it is calculated by taking an individual's rate of pay plus all expense payments and benefits provided in a year less pension fund contributions. For this purpose expenses covered by a dispensation are not excluded from the calculation, and all employments held by an individual within the same group of companies are treated as a single employment.

The completed returns should be submitted to the Inspector of Taxes by 6 May following the tax year end. Failure to submit a P11D, or submitting an incorrect P11D, can result in a charge to penalties.

CAN I CUT DOWN ON THE BURDEN OF COMPLETING P11DS?

Yes. Your Inspector of Taxes can issue you with a dispensation to cover certain of the expense sections of the P11D. This would mean that it would not be necessary to complete those sections of the P11D covered by the dispensation. The section most commonly included in dispensations is travelling and subsistence expenses, and such a dispensation can alleviate some of the administrative burden of P11D reporting. Before granting a dispensation the Inspector will need to be satisfied that the expenses to be covered in it are all allowable for tax purposes (section 198, ICTA 1988). However, a request for a dispensation can lead to the Inland Revenue carrying out a P11D compliance review and, for this reason, it is recommended that the employer initiates a review of procedures before approaching the Inspector. Once the dispensation has been issued, it will be important to keep the Inspector advised of any proposed changes to the expense reimbursement policies.

FOR WHICH EMPLOYEES DO I NEED TO SUBMIT A P9D?

A P9D return should be submitted to the Inland Revenue for employees either receiving expense payments totalling more than £25 per annum or receiving certain benefits where a P11D return is inappropriate because the P11D threshold has not been exceeded. A return should also be submitted for all directors for whom a P11D is not appropriate. The time limit and penalty provisions are the same as for P11D returns.

WHAT RECORDS DO I NEED TO KEEP FOR PAYE PURPOSES?

The PAYE regulations require the employer to retain for not less than three years all wages sheets, deductions working sheets, certificates and other documents and records relating to the calculation and payment of emoluments.

Inland Revenue compliance visits

WHICH INLAND REVENUE DEPARTMENTS CARRY OUT COMPLIANCE CHECKS?

Compliance checks are carried out by the following Inland Revenue departments:

- *the employer's own PAYE Tax District*   The District will normally carry out compliance checks in relation to P11D and P9D reporting requirements
- *a PAYE Audit Group*   These Groups carry out PAYE compliance checks of large employers and groups of companies
- *the Collector of Taxes*   The Collector will carry out PAYE compliance checks of smaller employers
- *a Special Office*   A comprehensive PAYE and P11D review can be carried out by a Special Office and this would normally be part of some other enquiry.

Apart from the Special Offices' compliance reviews, none of the other Inland Revenue departments would normally carry out a comprehensive review covering both the PAYE regulations and the P11D reporting requirements. The broad operational objectives of these different branches are the same, but the emphasis and conduct of the reviews vary.

We should mention the Board's Investigation Office. Although this unit does not carry out routine compliance checks, it does investigate cases where it is suspected that an offence has been committed against the Inland Revenue. These investigations would include cases of suspected fraud by contractors and sub-contractors in the construction industry.

WHAT POWERS DO THE INLAND REVENUE HAVE?

The PAYE regulations provide that the Inland Revenue can require an employer to produce for inspection at the employer's premises all wages sheets, deductions working sheets, certificates and other documents and records relating to the calculation and payment of emoluments.

WHAT CHECKS WILL BE CARRIED OUT ON THE VISIT?

An Inland Revenue department which carries out PAYE compliance checks will normally select a sample period from the last completed tax year. The records inspected will comprise the payroll and supporting documentation, as well as the records and vouchers which record and support expense payments to employees. If irregularities are identified, the Inland Revenue officer will request an estimate of the payment made under the relevant heading for past years. This is usually for the past six years in charge to tax. General questions can also be raised in relation to benefit matters, but the enquiry will not usually be as extensive as a review carried out by a Tax District P11D compliance team.

In contrast, the Tax District compliance teams, who are primarily concerned with carrying out compliance checks to ensure that the P11D and P9D reporting requirements have been met, normally question management in detail on the expense reimbursement policies operated and benefits provided to employees. By this process any area of under-disclosure can be identified. Where this happens, and the Inland Revenue consider that there is a loss of tax, the management will be requested to estimate the payments made for past years—again this will normally be the six years in charge.

HOW SHOULD MANAGEMENT REACT TO THE COMPLIANCE VISIT?

The Inland Revenue will normally announce their intention of carrying out a compliance check in writing and request convenient dates for the visit to take place. Management should prepare for the visit, and consider whether it is appropriate to take professional advice. The adviser will be able to explain the way in which the inspection visit will be conducted, and how it should be handled, discuss any areas of concern before the visit and make appropriate recommendations. We consider that a member of senior management should co-ordinate the visit and hold all meetings with Inland Revenue personnel. This will enable any questions raised by the Inland Revenue to be answered by somebody fully conversant with the company's policies. Depending on the circumstances it may be appropriate for the advisor to be present at these meetings.

Assessments

WILL THE INLAND REVENUE RAISE AN ASSESSMENT FOR UNPAID TAX?

In relation to PAYE the Inland Revenue have the power to raise an assessment on the employer in respect of unpaid PAYE tax and national insurance. However, in the first instance, the Inland Revenue will quantify their estimates of the underpaid tax and national insurance contributions and will normally attempt to reach a voluntary settlement with the employer. If this happens it is important to bring to bear the maximum experience of negotiating such settlements. Tax cases, Inland Revenue concessions and practice need to be considered to ensure that a settlement is reached which takes account of all relevant matters and mitigating factors.

The position in relation to P11D and P9D matters is different. So far as under-disclosure on Forms P11D and P9D is concerned, the employer is under no obligation to meet any tax liability arising. The Inland Revenue are entitled to have details of any under-disclosures, but the employer may of course be liable to a penalty. However, when under-disclosures arise, other considerations nearly always apply, for example the demotivating affect on employees if they have to pay the tax themselves. The employer should therefore consider whether a negotiated settlement is appropriate to prevent Inland Revenue assessing the employees to tax on benefits received in past tax years. Again it is important to take professional advice in this specialist area.

WHAT PENALTIES CAN I INCUR FOR NOT COMPLYING WITH THE REGULATIONS?

Offences committed prior to 27 July 1989

For offences committed prior to 27 July 1989 (the date of Royal Assent of the Finance Act 1989) the legislation provided for PAYE compliance failures based on documentary offences. Where an employer failed to make a return, give a certificate or produce a document or record in accordance with the regulations, he was liable to a penalty not exceeding £50 per documentary offence, and, if the penalty continued after a declaration by the Court or Commissioners, a further penalty not exceeding £10 per documentary offence for each day the penalty continued. If the employer fraudulently or negligently furnished or produced incorrect information, returns or certificates, he was liable to a penalty not exceeding £250 per documentary offence and, in the case of fraud, the penalty was £500. The Board of Inland Revenue could, at their discretion, mitigate these penalties.

Offences committed after 27 July 1989

The Finance Act 1989 introduced a new penalty régime for PAYE non-compliances, the full impact of which will not be felt until at least 1995. There are, however, transitional provisions which have an immediate impact.

The payment of PAYE for the last month of the tax year will continue to be due by 19 April following the tax year end. However, year end PAYE returns (ie P14, P35, P38 and P38A) will be due by 19 May following the tax year end. Previously these returns were also due by 19 April.

From 1995 at the earliest, failure to submit year end PAYE returns by the due date will attract, for a period up to 12 months, an automatic penalty of £100 per 50 employees per month. If the failure to make the returns continues beyond 12 months, the employer will be liable to an additional penalty of up to 100% of any tax unpaid at 19 April following the tax year in question.

In the transition period commencing 1989/90, the Inland Revenue will be entitled, in the case of failure to make the returns on time, to take proceedings before the Commissioners, who are empowered to award a penalty of up to £1,200 per 50 employees. For 1989/90 proceedings will not be taken where returns are submitted by 19 August 1990 and this deadline will be brought forward progressively for later years—becoming 19 May by 1995. If the failure continues after such initial penalty has been imposed, a further automatic penalty will arise £100 per 50 employees for each month (or part of a month) for the period up to 12 months from the date the returns were due. If the failure to submit the year end returns continues beyond 12 months, an additional maximum penalty of 100% of the tax due but unpaid can be levied.

From 1989/90 if the returns when submitted are incorrect the Inland Revenue can assess a further penalty of up to 100% of the tax underpaid as a result of the error but the total tax-geared penalties will never exceed 100% of the tax underpaid. Thus, if a return is submitted more than 12 months late and is subsequently found to be incorrect the total combined tax-geared penalties will not exceed 100% of the total tax underpaid.

Failure to submit P11D returns by the due date (6 May following the tax year end) will render the employer liable to an initial maximum penalty of £300 per return, plus an additional maximum penalty of £60 per return for each day the failure continues. The maximum penalty for the submission of an incorrect P11D return is increased to £3,000 with no distinction between negligent error and fraud.

IS THERE ANY INTEREST CHARGED FOR LATE PAID PAYE?

At present there is no general interest charge on late paid PAYE, but the Finance Act 1988 provided for an automatic interest charge to be introduced at a future date. This is not expected to be before 1993.

However, at present, in the exceptional circumstances where the Inland Revenue issue a Regulation 29 determination claiming from the employer PAYE tax should have been deducted, interest is charged from 14 days following the tax year for which the determination is raised. For example if the Inland Revenue issue a Regulation 29 determination in respect of 1988/89, interest will be charged for the period from 19 April 1989 to the date of payment of the tax. For determinations issued currently in respect of the years 1987/88 and earlier, interest runs from 20 April 1988 even though the determination is issued after that date.

Common problems

Here we cover some of the questions that commonly arise either as a result of an Inland Revenue compliance visit or when management seek clarification of the tax position of a particular transaction. Each situation must be judged on its own facts and circumstances; however we have tried to give a general indication of the tax position. In our answers we have, where applicable, referred to the differing tax treatments which apply to higher-paid and lower-paid employees.

IN ADDITION TO MY EMPLOYEES I USE THE SERVICES OF A NUMBER OF FREELANCERS AND CONSULTANTS AND PAY THEM AGAINST INVOICES WITHOUT DEDUCTION OF TAX AND NATIONAL INSURANCE. COULD THIS BE A PROBLEM?

Yes it can if the Inland Revenue subsequently determine that these individuals are, in fact, your employees. If this happens you may receive a claim in respect of the tax and national insurance contributions the Inland Revenue say you should have deducted. From the employer's point of view he should reduce the risk in this area as much as possible. The Inland Revenue state in the *Employer's Guide* that PAYE procedures should be operated if there is any doubt about the status of individuals. To safeguard the position the employer should obtain evidence to support the tax status of the individuals concerned. This can be done by verifying the payment is to an individual who has rendered a VAT invoice, and by obtaining documentary evidence that the Inland Revenue accept the individual as self-employed; for example by obtaining details of the person's Schedule D tax reference number. If the employer has any doubts after carrying out these checks reference should be made to the Inspector of Taxes.

MOST EMPLOYEES WORK AT THE HEAD OFFICE, BUT THERE ARE OCCASIONS WHEN EMPLOYEES ARE SECONDED TO WORK AT OTHER OFFICES AND LOCATIONS. AS THESE ARE NOT WITHIN REASONABLE COMMUTING DISTANCE OF OUR HEAD OFFICE, IS THERE ANY PROBLEM WITH PAYING FOR THE TRAVEL, ACCOMMODATION AND SUBSISTENCE COSTS INVOLVED?

An employee will not normally be taxed on reimbursed expenses to cover the reasonable additional travelling and subsistence costs incurred when he is required temporarily to work at a location away from his normal place of work. The Inland Revenue take the view that a temporary secondment is one lasting 12 months or less, but that once the secondment exceeds 12 months, or when it is known that it will exceed 12 months, any travel, accommodation or subsistence costs paid become taxable.

Problems arise, particularly in service industries, where employees spend a substantial amount of their time at client locations and very little and sometimes no time at their employer's office. In these situations it is important to agree the tax status of any payments with the Inspector of Taxes. In some circumstances it may be appropriate to contend that no tax charge should arise even though the employee spends substantial periods working at client locations.

I HAVE A NUMBER OF EMPLOYEES WHO OCCASIONALLY HAVE TO WORK AWAY
FROM THEIR OFFICE BASE. WHAT TRAVEL AND SUBSISTENCE PAYMENTS CAN I
MAKE AND WHAT ARE THE PAYE AND P11D/P9D REPORTING REQUIREMENTS?

Where the employer reimburses the actual costs incurred by the employee
this will not normally result in a tax charge. However where, as an alternative, the employer pays a fixed scale allowance, this should be cleared in
advance with the Inspector of Taxes, which would result in it being included
in the dispensation. If the allowance is not included in this way the Inland
Revenue could later take the view that it was a round sum allowance which
should have been paid through the payroll. In these circumstances they
could claim the tax and national insurance contributions, which should have
been deducted, from the employer.

SOMETIMES I REQUIRE MY EMPLOYEES TO WORK SO LATE THAT THERE IS NO
PUBLIC TRANSPORT AVAILABLE FOR THEM TO TRAVEL HOME. I PAY THE TAXI
FARES. IS THIS A PROBLEM?

These payments are in respect of home to office travel and are generally
taxable irrespective of their commercial justification. However, an extra-
statutory concession published in 1987 provides that, where an employee is
occasionally required to work late, and public transport has either ceased to
run or it would not be reasonable to expect the employee to use it, an income
tax liability will not arise. This concession only applies in certain specified
circumstances.

For home to office journeys the way in which the payment is made is
important in determining whether a national insurance liability arises.
Where it is a cash reimbursement to the employee the payment will be
subject to both tax (unless covered by the tax concessions) and national
insurance. However, where as an alternative the employer pays the taxi firm
direct, the amount may be considered a taxable benefit but no national
insurance charge will arise. Generally a benefit will only arise on an
employee who is higher paid for tax purposes.

WHEN I TAKE ON NEW EMPLOYEES OR REQUIRE EXISTING EMPLOYEES TO MOVE
THEIR JOB TO A NEW LOCATION I PAY ALL THE COSTS ARISING. I HAVE ALWAYS
ASSUMED THAT THERE IS NO QUESTION OF TAX LIABILITY, BUT IS THIS THE
CASE?

Payments to meet the costs of relocation are tax free under an Inland
Revenue concession, provided that they are 'reasonable in amount' and
'properly controlled'. The Inland Revenue does not define 'reasonable' in
this context, but, in practice, the reimbursement of any specifically incurred
expenditure, such as estate agents' fees, legal fees, etc, will not give rise to a
tax charge. Problems can arise where an employer pays a general disturbance allowance calculated as a percentage of salary. This will normally not
be accepted by the Inland Revenue, although they will accept that an
element of the disturbance allowance is tax free. To prevent a problem
arising later it is advisable to clear the relocation policy with the Inspector of
Taxes so that it is included in the dispensation.

Under an extra-statutory concession published in 1987 the employer can
also contribute towards the extra cost of a move to a higher cost area when

an employee is compulsorily transferred within the organisation. The concession lays down certain conditions which have to be satisfied.

I PAY A PERCENTAGE OF THE HOME TELEPHONE BILLS FOR CERTAIN OF MY EMPLOYEES, AS I NEED THEM TO BE ON CALL OUTSIDE WORKING HOURS, AND FROM TIME TO TIME THEY WILL NEED TO MAKE BUSINESS CALLS. IS THERE ANY PROBLEM?

Income tax

The amount paid for business calls will not normally give rise to a tax charge but should be disclosed on Form P11D unless covered by a dispensation. The tax position on rental payments is different. The Inland Revenue's view is that any element of the rental paid by the employer is not wholly, exclusively and necessarily incurred in the performance of the employee's duties and is therefore taxable in full. However, by concession, some element of the rental may be accepted by the Inland Revenue as tax free in emergency call-out situations.

National insurance

As regards national insurance, no charge will arise where the employer is the subscriber. However, where the employee is the subscriber and the telephone is used for both business and private purposes the full rental will be subject to national insurance contributions. In relation to business calls paid by the employer (where the employee is the subscriber) a national insurance charge will arise unless the reimbursement is supported by details of the individual business calls made.

OCCASIONS DO ARISE WHEN I DEEM IT NECESSARY FOR MY WIFE TO TRAVEL WITH ME ON AN OVERSEAS BUSINESS TRIP AND THE COMPANY PAYS THE COSTS ARISING. IS THERE ANY PROBLEM?

Where travel and subsistence costs have been paid by the employer in relation to a spouse of a director or higher-paid employee, there should be a disclosure of the costs attributable to the spouse on the employee's P11D. It is unlikely that these costs would be covered by a dispensation, as it is normal Inland Revenue practice for such costs to be specifically excluded. It is then for the employee to claim a deduction for the expenses on his own tax return. Each trip would be judged on the facts, but it is possible that the Inspector will agree to apportion the costs where the wife has carried out some business functions on the trip.

IF A COMPANY PROVIDES MEALS FOR ALL STAFF, IS THERE A PROBLEM IF THE DIRECTORS HAVE A SEPARATE LUNCH FACILITY AS, ON SOME DAYS, THEY WILL ENTERTAIN CUSTOMERS AND OTHER VISITORS?

Where an employer provides meals to all employees a benefit will not normally arise. However, the provision of a separate facility for the directors may give rise to an Inland Revenue contention that a benefit arises if the cost of it is significantly greater than the costs of the other facilities. The extent of any benefit is not easy to quantify, and many factors need to be taken into account, including the extent to which the facilities are used for entertaining. The costs in relation to entertaining undertaken in the facility should of course be disallowed for corporation tax purposes.

WHERE SPECIAL CLOTHING AND UNIFORMS ARE PROVIDED FOR EMPLOYEES TO WEAR AT WORK DOES A TAX CHARGE ARISE?

Generally the Inland Revenue regard the provisions of clothing to employees as taxable. However, where protective clothing or uniforms are provided, the Inland Revenue may agree that no taxable benefit arises. For a uniform to be accepted it will normally have to display the company logo or some other identification mark in a prominent position. Where a cash contribution for clothing is made by the employer, it is likely that the Inland Revenue would contend that a liability to both tax and national insurance arises.

WHERE INCENTIVES ARE PROVIDED BY WAY OF HOLIDAYS, MERCHANDISE AND VOUCHERS TO BOTH EMPLOYEES AND TO THIRD PARTIES, HOW CAN THE PROVIDER MEET THE TAX LIABILITIES ARISING?

In 1984 the Inland Revenue set up an Incentive Valuation Unit to be responsible for co-ordinating the collection of tax on incentive awards. The awards can take the form of holidays, vouchers exchangeable for goods or services or items of merchandise. The Inland Revenue have published their view on the valuation of awards and will enter into contractual arrangements for the provider to pay the basic rate tax in relation to both his own employees and the employees of third parties. Practical difficulties arise to providers who wish to meet the total tax liabilities of the recipients of the incentives given, and it is therefore important to consider all tax aspects of an Incentive Award Scheme before any awards are made.

The Inland Revenue have published two press releases which may be relevant in considering the tax implications of incentive schemes. The first concerns legislation (section 155(7), ICTA 1988) exempting entertainment provided to an employee of a third party. The second concerns an extra-statutory concession exempting gifts provided to an employee of a third party. A tax liability will not arise on the recipient in respect of these items in certain specified circumstances.

VAT Considerations

Introduction

VAT is both complex and subject to frequent changes. There are, however, often areas for improvement and cost saving in the way that a business approaches its VAT affairs. In addition, the consequences of failure to comply with VAT regulations, in terms of additional liabilities, surcharges, penalties and interest charges can be severe. Many of the topics dealt with in this section are of concern to all companies, irrespective of their size, and some cover fairly basic concepts. Nevertheless there is a particular danger that the growth of a company will not be matched by an increased awareness that additional management resources must be allocated to monitoring the effectiveness of VAT accounting procedures.

Groups

Where the business has grown to the point where it operates within a group structure, then management may wish to take advantage of a 'group registration' for VAT purposes.

Two (or more) companies may be 'grouped' for VAT purposes if they are resident in the UK or have UK resident directors and if one is controlled by the other or both are controlled by a third party. The control of the companies grouped does *not* have to be established in the UK.

The advantage of group registration is that supplies between members of the group are disregarded for VAT purposes. However, all members of a VAT group are jointly and severally liable for the group's VAT whilst they are in that VAT group. Furthermore, a former group company continues to be liable for tax due during its period of membership even after it leaves the group.

Customs & Excise have the power to refuse grouping in certain circumstances and they will examine all applications for group registration where the motive is clearly to avoid VAT.

Partial exemption

Input tax incurred in making taxable supplies is recoverable, whereas input tax incurred in making non-taxable supplies is not. Businesses which make only non-taxable supplies cannot therefore register for VAT.

Businesses which make a mixture of taxable and non-taxable supplies are known as 'partially exempt'. Such businesses must apportion the recovery of their input tax between exempt and taxable supplies. The 'standard method' allows the company to recover input tax solely attributable to taxable supplies; input tax solely attributable to non-taxable supplies is of course irrecoverable. The business must ascertain how much input tax cannot be attributed solely to taxable or non-taxable supplies. This is known as 'residual input tax'. The standard method allows the recovery of part of the residual input tax, equivalent to the same percentage as the input tax incurred on taxable supplies to total input tax. Businesses whose 'exempt input tax' (ie the input tax attributable directly and indirectly to non-taxable supplies) falls below certain monthly 'de minimis' limits are entitled to ignore them and accordingly recover all of the input tax they have incurred. The present 'de minimis' limits are £100 per month on average; or both £250 per month on average and 50% of all input tax; or both £500 per month on average and 25% of all input tax.

In many instances the 'standard method' is not to a business' advantage and it may be possible to agree a special partial exemption method with Customs & Excise. Such special methods include using an output based, rather than an input based calculation, reference to how much floor space a business uses in making taxable supplies or any other methods which Customs & Excise may approve. Using an appropriate 'special' partial exemption method is one of the most likely means by which a partially exempt business can make substantial savings of VAT. It is therefore important that within such a business organisation there is a member of the management team who has a clear responsibility for monitoring the partial exemption position, especially so where the business is operating close to the 'de minimis' limit of exempt input tax.

The business should also monitor any changes in structure or trading style that may affect the special method authorisation. Even if the changes do not lead to withdrawal of the method by Customs, they may mean that the method in use is no longer the most economic and should be revised.

The capital goods scheme

With effect from 1 April 1990, it is necessary to adjust input tax claims relating to computers valued at £50,000 or more, and buildings valued at £250,000 or more over a five year period (ten years in the case of buildings). If a relevant capital item was bought for a solely exempt use, then no input tax paid on its purchase would be recoverable. If during the five or ten year period of adjustment, the capital item was used wholly or in part for a taxable purpose, then some of that previously irrecoverable VAT would be recoverable. (Customs & Excise will only apply these provisions to acquisitions made *after* 1 April 1990 as before that date they are not 'capital items' as defined in the legislation.)

This scheme is likely to lead to an increased burden of administration as a result of the need to keep records in order to operate the scheme where the user company is making some exempt supplies. It should be possible to avoid this administrative burden by arranging for high value computers and buildings to be acquired by a company (which would have to be separately registered for VAT) which makes taxable supplies of the assets under operating leases (in the case of computers) or by granting a lease subject to the option to tax (in the case of buildings) to the user company. In this way all of the input tax incurred in acquiring the capital items should be recoverable, but a VAT cost will arise as some of the VAT which will be charged by the leasing company is likely to be irrecoverable by the partially exempt user company. This cost can be minimised with careful planning.

International services

The business should ensure that it has correctly treated services supplied to overseas customers or supplies from overseas suppliers. Most, but not all, services supplied by businesses resident in the UK to persons outside the UK are zero-rated. If zero-rating is incorrectly applied, VAT costs and, possibly penalties and interest charges may arise.

Certain services supplied by a party resident outside the UK to a business resident in the UK are subject to a 'reverse charge'. These services are set out in Schedule 3, Value Added Tax Act 1983. They include:

- services of consultants, engineers, consulting bureaux, lawyers, accountants and other similar services; data processing and provision of information (but excluding any services relating to land)
- banking, financial and insurance services.

The practical consequence of the reverse charge is that a VAT registered business must account for VAT on such services as if it had itself made the supply. Output tax is calculated on the amount paid to the supplier. The same amount should be recovered as input tax. A partially exempt business will be able to recover that input tax only subject to its recovery rate under its partial exemption method.

A business which is not registered for VAT (for example, one which makes only exempt supplies) may be liable to register and account for VAT on services which it imports if their value exceeds the VAT turnover threshold.

Pension funds

Pension funds are not eligible to register separately for VAT, unless they are making taxable supplies. Such supplies could be the freehold sale of new commercial property, or receiving rentals from commercial property developments on which the option to tax has been exercised, or making sales of securities to non-EC persons. For VAT purposes, some of the expenses of a pension fund may be regarded as relating to the employer's business. VAT on expenses incurred in establishing the fund and in its day-to-day administration is treated as part of the employer's costs and is recoverable provided that he receives invoices addressed to him (and not to the fund, fund manager or trustees). Input tax on the trustees' expenses, such as investment advice, is not recoverable by the employer.

If they are registered, most pension funds will be partially exempt as their investment income will be a mixture of exempt and taxable supplies. It is therefore important for the fund to determine the most advantageous method for input tax recovery.

Implications of mergers, reconstructions and takeovers

The purchase or sale of a business or company will usually have VAT implications—whether the transaction is part of a reorganisation within a group of companies or a disposal/acquisition to/from a third party.

Transfers of going concerns

The 'transfer' (sale) of a business as a going concern is outside the scope of VAT. Thus, tax must not be charged on the transfer by the vendor. If tax is incorrectly charged on a tax invoice, the vendor would have to account for the VAT charged while the purchaser would be unable to treat the tax paid as input tax. Clearly it can be beneficial to take advantage of the Transfer of Going Concern (TOGC) provisions where the purchaser is an exempt or partially exempt supplier since if VAT had to be charged on the transfer it could be irrecoverable in whole or in part.

To be a transfer of a going concern:

- the business or part of a business must be capable of independent operation as a going concern
- it must be operating at the time of transfer and continue with no significant break
- if the transferor is registered for VAT the business must be transferred to a person who is or will become liable to register for VAT
- the purchaser must continue to operate the *same* kind of business, if only for a short period.

Going concerns—the reverse charge on partly exempt purchasers

The purchaser of a 'going concern' is, however, required to account for VAT on the value of assets transferred if it is a company which is part of a VAT group and the VAT group is or becomes partly exempt in the VAT year in which the transfer occurs.

Registration

The transfer of a business can create a liability for the transferee to register (where, for instance, as a result of the acquisition the purchaser is taken above the threshold for registration). Alternatively, even where registration by the transferee is not strictly required, it could nevertheless be advantageous if it meant that the transfer would qualify under the TOGC provisions.

It is not only the transfer of a business that can create a requirement to register. The transfer of a company that was previously part of a group registration could also require that steps be taken to register it, either in its own right or as part of another VAT group.

The sale of a company from a VAT group will require the vendor to notify Customs & Excise of the changes, so that the company can be excluded from the VAT group from the date of the sale. The purchaser will have to take steps either to obtain separate registration for the company or to include it in another VAT Group if the company is making taxable supplies above the registration thresholds.

The penalty for failure to notify a liability to register is between 10% and 30% of any net tax payable during the period that the default continues. If such a default occurs, the only way of avoiding the penalty is to demonstrate that there was a reasonable excuse for the failure to notify.

Warranties and indemnities

In merger and takeover situations, it is important for the purchaser to consider VAT penalties or liabilities that may arise from the vendor's period of ownership. From 1 April 1990 Customs & Excise will be able to charge interest on tax recovered or recoverable by assessment even in cases where a company discovers an underdeclaration itself and pays the outstanding sum. A serious misdeclaration penalty will be imposed on top of interest when more substantial errors have occurred, but this is waived if a voluntary disclosure is made prior to Customs' enquiries being made. Clearly, it is important that VAT reviews are undertaken prior to acquisition and mergers, particularly in the area of compliance; and warranties and indemnities should be drafted to cover all potential VAT penalty and liability situations.

Penalties, surcharges and interest—Finance Act 1985

As a result of provisions enacted in the Finance Act 1985 and introduced in stages between 25 July 1985 and 1 April 1990 Customs & Excise are now able to impose stringent surcharges and penalties on businesses that commit a wide range of VAT offences, including the unauthorised issue of a VAT invoice, failing to notify a liability to register for VAT on time, failing to submit a VAT return or pay the VAT due with it on time, making a serious misdeclaration of VAT and dishonestly evading VAT. From 1 April 1990 Customs & Excise will also be able to charge interest on overdue VAT.

The management of the growing company should ensure that the VAT recording and settlement systems develop in line with the growth in the business if the threat of substantial penalties is to be minimised.

Index

Accounting information systems. *See also* COMPUTERISED MANAGEMENT INFORMATION SYSTEMS; MANAGEMENT INFORMATION SYSTEMS
  activities associated with sub-systems, 35–36
  components of, 29, 34–35
  functioning of, 34
  nature of, 33
Acquisition
  company of. *See* CORPORATE ACQUISITIONS
Added value logistics. *See also* CUSTOMER SERVICE
  friendly design, 113
  generally, 111
  market sector, logistics by, 113–114
  order penetration point, moving, 111–113
  priority allocation rules, 114
  sales agents, managing, 113
Advance corporation tax (ACT)
  loss of surplus, disallowance of, 86
Advertising
  marketing mix, as factor of, 101–102
Advisors
  role of, 2
Agencies
  recruitment, 126–127
Agents
  sales, managing, 113
Allocation
  priority allocation rules, 114
Assets
  disposals, timing of, 78
  net asset basis of valuation of target company, 138–139

Bills of exchange
  nature and advantages of, 67–68
Bonus schemes
  deferred remuneration schemes, 91
  generally, 90, 129
  profit related pay, 90–91
Brand
  values, as factor on which positioning may be based, 99
Buildings in Enterprise Zones
  tax efficient investment, as, 76
Business
  acquisition of. *See* CORPORATE ACQUISITIONS
  plan. *See* BUSINESS PLAN

Business Expansion Scheme (BES)
  tax efficient investment, as, 76
Business plan. *See also* CORPORATE PLANNING
  advantages of, 19
  detail required in, 19–20
  need for, 19
  preparation of, general tips on, 24–25
  structure of—
    appendices, 24
    funding requirement, 24
    future trading, 23–24
    generally, 20
    introduction/executive summary, 20–21
    management, 22
    market/competition, 22–23
    operation/products/service, 21
    past trading, 22–23

Capital
  development capital distinguished from venture capital, 59
  goods scheme, VAT in relation to, 161–162
  losses, planning for, 87–88
  venture. *See* VENTURE CAPITAL
  working, management of. *See* WORKING CAPITAL MANAGEMENT
Capital gains tax
  planning, 74
Capital tax. *See also* TAX PLANNING
  planning, 73
City Grant Scheme
  features of, 144–145
  urban programme areas, 149
Company
  acquisition of. *See* CORPORATE ACQUISITIONS
Competition. *See also* MARKET; MARKETING
  analysis of industry and, 7–16
  assessment of, by venture capital investor, 62
  business plan, market/competition in, 21–22
  competitive advantage—
    achievement of, 7
    importance of, 6
    sustaining—
      cost, 93
      generally, 92, 94–95
      market access, 92
      product, 92